*Sun Dogs & Eagle Down*

# SUN DOGS & EAGLE DOWN

## The Indian Paintings of Bill Holm

*by* STEVEN C. BROWN

*Chronology & Bibliography*

*by* LLOYD J. AVERILL

*Captions by* BILL HOLM

*The University of Washington Press / Seattle & London*

*Douglas & McIntyre / Vancouver & Toronto*

*Sun Dogs and Eagle Down: The Indian Paintings of Bill Holm* is published with the assistance of a grant from the University of Washington Press Editor's Endowment, supported through the generosity of Janet and John Creighton, Patti Knowles, Mary McLellan Williams, and other donors.

Library of Congress Cataloging-in-Publication Data

Brown, Steven C.
Sun dogs & eagle down : the Indian paintings of Bill Holm / by Steven C. Brown ; chronology & bibliography by Lloyd J. Averill ; captions by Bill Holm.
p.   cm.
Includes bibliographical references.
ISBN 0-295-97947-X (cloth)
1. Holm, Bill, 1925 — Criticism and interpretation.   2. Indians in art.
3. Indians of North America — Pictorial works.   I. Title: Sun dogs and eagle down.
II. Holm, Bill, 1925–   III. Averill, Lloyd J. (Lloyd James), 1923–   IV. Title.
ND237.H66948 B76   2000
759.13 — dc21                           00-021618

Canadian Cataloguing in Publication Data

Brown, Steven C.
Sun dogs & eagle down

Includes bibliographical references.
ISBN 1-55054-777-1

1. Holm, Bill, 1925–   2. Indians of North America in art.   I. Averill, Lloyd J. (Lloyd James), 1923–   II. Holm, Bill, 1925–
III. Title.
ND237.H66948B76   2000
                    759.13    C00-910144-6

# Contents

# COLOR PLATES

# *Preface*

T O   A T T E M P T   A   B O O K   O N   B I L L   H O L M ,   O R   E V E N   O N   A   S I N G L E   F A C E T of his multiply talented personality, is a little like doing a book on the Pacific Ocean — it just keeps getting deeper! Short of creating an illustrated tome covering all of his many interests, past contributions, and ongoing projects, we have chosen in this volume to focus on Bill Holm the painter. Since his retirement from academic and curatorial duties in 1985, Bill's central passion has been the painting of historical images of the Northwest Coast, Plains, and Plateau First Peoples. And because such art is meant to be widely seen and enjoyed as a rich repository of information, to be shared when possible beyond the circle of its collectors, he has, for once, felt relatively comfortable with the limelight. But only relatively so. Known far and wide for being extremely generous in sharing his time, knowledge, and experience, Bill is also a very private person, deeply committed to his family and to those activities most important to them. A dedicated and humble individual, he had to be urged repeatedly to become the subject of a book. He was not inclined to have a volume produced in his name that might strive to elevate his image above the many other very talented artists involved in his several chosen fields.

It is clear to us how and why he might feel this way. Sculptor and art historian Steve Brown has been a close friend and colleague of Bill's since not long after their first meeting in 1966. He has worked and spent time with Bill and his family for untold hours over the years, assisting with various of Bill's projects like the building of his studio from the ground up, from clearing the land to carving the interior. Writer and collector Lloyd Averill, a faculty colleague at the University of Washington, has taken all of Bill's major courses, has participated in years of formal and informal workshops under Bill's instruction, and has been a personal friend of the Holms since 1984. To both of us it is always apparent that Bill's creative motivation is based on the pure doing of any enterprise. He strives to learn, to discover, to educate. In no way is he interested in impressing other people with his accomplishments. His accomplishments, therefore, must speak for themselves.

Serendipitously, and because it has become his central focus, Bill's career as a painter also encompasses many of his other pursuits, most of which interrelate with his anthropological and technical research and his background of creativity, thereby serving to bring remarkable accuracy and historical presence to his work. In focusing on this most recent facet of his career, we mean not to ignore the other sides of his broad-ranging persona, but merely to home in on one important part that speaks clearly for the whole. Many people who have been aware for years of Bill Holm's scholarship and curatorial activities do not know of him as a painter. All those to whom this volume serves as an introduction will recognize at once the knowledge and the careful mastery of detail that he brings to his imagery, and the characteristic vitality with which he infuses his historical subject matter.

We have been happily blessed to work closely with Bill and Marty Holm during the development of this project and to receive valuable input as well from their daughters, Carla Holm Martens and Karen Holm, and his sister, Betty Holm Odle. In addition, Bill's own commentary on his paintings enriches this book in a way that none other can.

Lloyd Averill gratefully acknowledges the following people who gave time for interviews in preparation for the biographical chronology: Donn Charnley, Joe David, Robert Davidson, Barry Herem, Jack Hudson, Nathan Jackson, Aldona Jonaitis, Marvin Oliver, Duane and Katie Pasco, Bill and Martine Reid, Cheryl Samuel, Judge Alfred Scow, Henry Seaweed, David Stephens, and Robin Wright.

We also wish to express our appreciation to the collectors of Bill Holm's works for their generosity in sharing their treasured paintings. We hope sincerely that this introduction to Bill Holm's painting is as enjoyable for the reader to experience as it was for us to research, assemble, and write.

STEVEN C. BROWN
*Salmon Bay, Washington*

LLOYD J. AVERILL
*Seattle, Washington*

*Sun Dogs & Eagle Down*

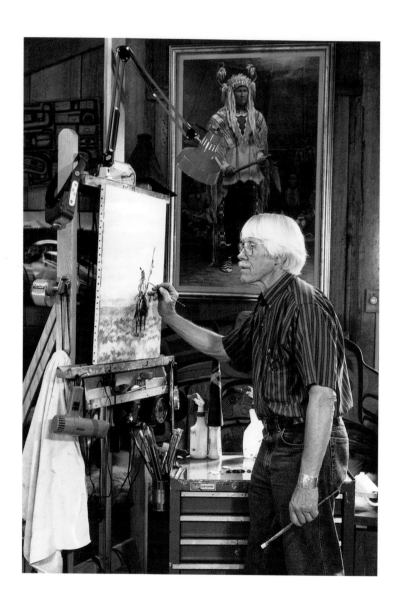

*Bill Holm in his studio (Photo by Marcia Iverson)*

# Sun Dogs & Eagle Down:

# The Indian Paintings of Bill Holm

## STEVEN C. BROWN

THIS COLLECTION OF PICTURES BY BILL HOLM ILLUSTRATES
a working career that until his academic retirement in 1985 was very much a
part-time avocation, a beloved pursuit that of necessity took a back seat to the
more immediate requirements of family, scholarship, and teaching. The series of images
herein begins with work produced in the 1950s, contains a few images that date in the
1960s and seventies, and then picks up with enthusiasm and increased focus following
his family's maturation and his formal retirement from Burke Museum and University
of Washington positions. Though the years before 1985 allowed little opportunity for the
time commitment of brush and canvas, Holm's pens and pencils (and occasionally watercolors) were seldom still. Untold numbers of postal envelopes (a sampling of which
is reproduced here in figures 1–14), napkins and place mats, performance programs and
meeting agendas, have served as the spontaneous surfaces on which he projected his
artistic nature. Whether he was working out a design or an engineering challenge for a
specific project, or visually tinkering with different ideas for some future composition, or
just savoring the meditation of movement and the love of beauty and form, the creative
edge of his personality was always honed sharp, ready for immediate use.

It is hard to describe the thrill of receiving a correspondence from Bill Holm on
which he has penciled or penned the sketch of some miniaturized scene, usually related
to the content of the letter, thereby turning the envelope itself into something to be treasured. Two such delicious surprises have arrived in my mailbox: I received the first in

1978 in Neah Bay, Washington, when I was working with Makah carver Lance Wilkie on a 32-foot whaling canoe for the Makah Cultural and Research Center (figure 7). Using a felt tip pen, Holm has quickly sketched the scene of a whaling crew on the hunt. Six paddlers and the steersman are at work, deftly guiding their canoe through the waves. They appear to be nearing the final approach in the wake of a surface-breathing whale, unseen in the picture. The harpooner stands at the ready in the bow, the long hunting shaft and harpoon line poised as he surveys his relationship to their quarry.

The second treasure reached me in Tofino, British Columbia, while I was collaborating from a distance with Bill on the carving of a set of two Xwexwe masks for a family leader in Alert Bay (figure 9). The envelope displays the shaded pencil drawing of a nineteenth-century Kwakwaka'wakw artist at work on the beach. He is leaning against a split-and-adzed plank backrest, with his elbow adze beside him and a carpet of wood shavings beneath his feet, knifing in the details of a nearly completed Xwexwe mask cradled in his lap. It is easy to see Holm's fascination with each of these moments: the sleek, sure lines of the canoe as it glides through the water on this most perilous and spiritually sacred pursuit; the look of intent on the face of the mask carver as his manifestation of a powerful, unseen spirit is tooled into existence. Not content simply to enjoy such reflections privately in his own mind's eye, Holm's creative nature draws him to manifest these thoughts, even on such humble surfaces, so they can be known and appreciated by those who share his love of such imagery and the highly respected events of the past.

The paintings of Bill Holm represent but one of the many avenues of expression and creativity that this prolific artist and scholar has explored in his inspiring and highly energized career. It would seem that many lifetimes of knowledge and experience are embodied in this gentle and unassuming man. His voluminous output of creativity, information, and innovation tempts one to imagine that a whole collection of spirits resides in this single human form, each responsible for one of the bright facets that combine to make up the visible surface of his life. The number of paintings in this volume is relatively small, but each is a window into the remarkable experiential background from which the images emerge, suggesting the complex fabric of the personality that is the underlying foundation of each canvas.

When we first proposed this book to Bill Holm, he characteristically declined. He brought out a twelve-inch stack of coffee-table books on painters in the Western genre, and remarked that, in his opinion, "each one of these artists is a far better painter that I am!" Though Holm himself may feel outclassed by the technical skills he sees in the work of other painters, there is little doubt that it is extremely difficult to surpass his work in terms of its overall vision: the intimate feeling that he brings to each scene, the innate

1 / *An unadorned view of a Crow man of the northern Plains. Sent to Norman Feder. January 27, 1958. Colored pencil*

2 / *Canoes covered for sun protection before a village of Kwakwa̱ka'wakw houses. Sent to Norman Feder. 1964. Felt pen and wash, with white gouache*

familiarity with time and place and with the many intriguing pieces of history and life on which he focuses in each canvas. He is respected and esteemed internationally as a master of his chosen genre, for both his unparalleled knowledge of Native American material culture, and the passion for accuracy he brings to bear in his scholarship and his paintings. There is no question that he does something wonderful in his work, and his acknowledged authority is high among a broad cross section of ethnographic scholars, First Nations artists, Native American hobbyists, and other contemporary painters in the field of historic re-creation. Perhaps the special qualities he brings to his work are best recognized by those who are also experienced in and knowledgeable about the subjects that fall within his vision, but they captivate the uninitiated viewer just as soundly.

The verity of firsthand experience is readily apparent in Holm's paintings. He has seen the channels, inlets, villages, and shores of the Northwest Coast from the seat of a kayak, a sailboat, or a dugout canoe. Having observed the movements of paddlers, dancers, mask makers, horse people, singers, and craftspeople of many of the First Nations of the Northwest and the northern plains, he is able to draw upon familiar sights, sounds, and feelings that bring a fresh and natural sensibility to every scene. He knows the glow of firelight in a big-house, the shrouding of fog on the shoreline, the tinkle of small waves on beach gravel, the hospitality of a tipi fire, and he is able to represent each of these as naturally and spontaneously as we all produce the miracle of speech.

A handful of photographers in the nineteenth century managed to attain his style of documentation — some work by Curtis, Pratt, Winter & Pond, and others. But all were limited in those days by the relatively slow technological development of portable equipment and more sensitive film emulsions, by the types of subjects and cultural opportunities with which they were presented, and by their own artistic skills, vision, and ethnographic knowledge. In the privacy and timeless quiet of his studio, Bill Holm has been able to draw upon his personal experiences in the worlds of the First Peoples as well as his knowledge of historic traditions and technologies, and to muster his innate skill in visualizing the appropriate imageries with which to assemble these various aspects. As a result, scenes and events that were missed in the visual documents of the past can be pieced back together, reconstructed in lines and colors that more permanently manifest the spirits and images of the times. Some such moments took place in the past only once, while others were observed again and again, but most were not recorded in any location except the mind's eye and the memories of the living participants. Holm's paintings recapture the elements that these individuals once perceived and marveled at, and he brings them back to light that we all might learn from them of the beauty and visual magic that the unforgiving conflicts of cultures wrested from us prematurely.

6

3 / US Postal Service stamp honoring
*Chief Joseph of the Nez Perce (Nimipoo).*
*Holm's painting extends and completes*
*the portrait image printed on the stamp,*
*the border of which remains like a picture*
*frame. Joseph is holding a pipe tomahawk,*
*wearing a Plateau/transmontane beaded*
*shirt with ermine tubes, beaded cloth*
*leggings fringed with buckskin, and a*
*breechclout of Pendleton wool. Sent to*
*Norman Feder. 1965. Watercolor*

4 / *Strong profile of a Tsimshian clan*
*leader dressed in a mountain goat wool*
*dancing blanket and an ermine headdress*
*with frontlet. Sent to Norman Feder.*
*April 1973. Lithograph pencil*

Norman Feder
The Denver Art Museu
100 West 14th Avenue
Denver, Colorado 80

Bill Holm's obvious fascination with the people and the historic periods that he represents is born not of a romanticized retrospection, but rather of a profound respect for the individuals, the cultures, the historical situations, and the realities of those times. To speak with him of the worlds represented in these images quickly reveals the wonder and admiration that underlie his preoccupation with his subjects. His guiding inspiration clearly has been the strength and ingenuity of the First Peoples and their cultures as a whole, as well as a sense of wonderment and fascination with the physical trappings and artistic creations that evolved with them over time. His admiration is tempered with a respectful sense of honesty and truth. Nothing that doesn't belong within the culture or the moment is to be seen in the picture. We never see the wrong style of weapons in the hands of warriors, the inappropriate type of beads or design patterns on a shirt or leggings, or the lines of a canoe hull inaccurately drawn or represented in the wrong context. And yet this seeming obsession with detail never becomes overbearing or pedantic, never seems to take precedence over capturing the essence of the moment. Each is a historic dramatization, true to its place and time, whether the subjects are dressed in cotton shirts, wool pants, draped in a commercial wool shawl, or decked out in full traditional regalia of brain-tanned, quilled and beaded shirt, moccasins, and leggings. Such details are not the concern of many who work in this genre, perhaps because they are primarily painters, and not historians or scholars of art and culture who also paint. For Bill Holm, the detail is a natural and inextricable part of the scene. He knows what does and does not belong in the picture, and he would not be personally satisfied if all the parts of the whole were not true and appropriate to the subject, the time, and the specific place. The evidence of this perspective is everywhere in his pictures, becoming stronger as his artistic vision and sense of purpose have matured over time.

One of the most enriching and extraordinary aspects of Bill Holm's approach to his subjects is contained in that part of his creative life which does not directly involve brush and canvas but is an inseparable facet of the background of each painting. His daily life can be characterized as an ongoing research project, and his many experiences and tinkerings with Native materials and techniques, his creation of finished pieces that are the fruition of his curiosity and study, all bear importantly on the content and subject matter of his canvases. Any look at Bill Holm the painter must also incorporate the inquisitive experimenter, the masterful woodworker, the hide tanner, the bead and quill worker, the canoe maker — for the practical experience and knowledge gleaned from each of these pursuits is indelibly woven into the images of each picture. He is aware not only intellectually of the proper type of animal skin that was traditionally employed for a given garment or piece of equipment, or the appropriate styles of beaded or quilled designs used by a particular First Nation in a given time, or the correct style of Northwest Coast

5 / *On a stormy day, three northern Northwest Coast Indians sail their thirty-foot canoe through a windswept channel. Sent to Norman Feder. July 1977. Watercolor*

6 / *An Upper Missouri chief in his finery, holding a large-bladed trade hatchet. Sent to Hermann VonBank. November 1992. Watercolor*

7 / *A crew of Makah or Nuu-chah-nulth whalers moves in with the rhythm of the whale, on their approach for the harpoon strike. Sent to Steve Brown. July 1978. Felt pen*

design for a region and time period. He has in fact brain-tanned that skin, made that garment, or quiver, or stirrup; he knows every individual stitch of the bead or quill work that decorates the surface; and he has carved the masks, the canoes, built a Kwakwaka'wakw big-house (for Camp Nor'wester on Lopez Island) and a Haida-style house (as his studio), and painted or carved in nearly every two-dimensional style known from the Northwest Coast.

Many of these projects were undertaken just to see where the varied processes would lead. Some came about in order to realize the answers to questions inherent in the appreciation of a piece of work or material. How were the sheep horn bowls, ladles, and rattles really made? What happens when you steam a horn bowl, or a canoe hull, and open it out in the traditional manner? How do the traditional tools themselves influence the outcome of a particular carved form? Holm is usually not satisfied to accept a secondhand explanation of a process or technique, especially if his experienced logic sees some fault or discrepancy in a verbal or written account. He simply wants to know the truth of the matter, and is inclined to question for it, in order to avoid unnecessarily repeating the mistakes or misunderstandings of others.

A beadworker since he was ten years old, he has since produced pieces in a wide variety of styles and techniques and has written scholarly articles that have helped to clarify not only the processes and techniques themselves, but also the chronology, history, and tribal distribution of designs and techniques. A carver in the Northwest Coast style since he was a teenager, he has made at least one example of a great many of the archetypal Northwest Coast artworks—headdress frontlets, rattles, objects made of sheep or goat horn, argillite pieces, masks from nearly all areas and styles (including mechanical ones, in which he especially excels), four canoes (from eleven to thirty-five feet in length), totem poles in many styles, and metalwork.

These pieces were made not for mere entertainment, or for profitable sale, or for self-advancement in the field of contemporary Native arts, but with the primary goal of understanding the work, on a direct and personal basis, from the inside out. Not content to accept without question the statements of past ethnographers or historians on designs or techniques, he has tried a great many of them himself. He has learned what does or does not work and has rewritten the studies on many individual subjects, or encouraged his students and associates to carry forward with an idea for a personal study or an academic thesis. A glance at Bill Holm's list of publications reveals the richness and depth of his own scholarly artistic studies, each of which he has pursued with the simple agenda of knowing, experiencing, and appreciating the detail, the step-by-step process, and the actual feel of each differing material and approach to creation. Most of the pieces he has made in this way are still in his family's possession, gracing the walls of their home or his

8 / *A Haida artist of the late nineteenth century at work on an argillite pipe. The massive stern of his canoe forms the backdrop. This canoe is based directly on the thirty-five-foot canoe that Holm carved and painted in 1968. Painted for Robin Wright on the endpaper of* Analysis of Form. *1979. Acrylic*

9 / *A Kwakwa̱ka̱'wakw carver works at his backrest, knifing in the details of a Xwexwe mask on the day of the potlatch. Sent to Steve Brown. January 1980. Pencil*

studio. Others were made at the Henderson Camps/Camp Nor'wester for the enrichment of their youth programs, or for public education through displays in the Burke Museum and his University of Washington classes. Innumerable individuals, through the encounter of Bill Holm's work, have grown immensely in their appreciation for the art, technologies, and cultures of the Northwest Coast and Plateau First Nations. He is ever the willing teacher, and each of his creations is the touchstone to a long and enthusiastic story of how it came to be, the challenges encountered, and the discoveries made along the way. Many of these objects, made over a period of numerous years, have since become part of the painted record of Holm's work, to be discovered in each canvas. Others were made specifically as studies for particular paintings, so that each object's unique forms, its appearance in drapery or at particular angles, and its other special aspects could be properly represented in a two-dimensional format using oil, casein (for the earlier pieces), or acrylic paints.

In many of Bill Holm's paintings, the setting of the historical scene or the particular geographic location is as important to the full understanding of the picture as is an appreciation for the technical aspects or imagery involved. For this reason, each of the forty-nine paintings in this book is accompanied by Holm's own description of the contextual background for each scene. His words succinctly set the stage for each picture, or reveal its historical context — the chain of events leading up to the particular moment being depicted.

Beyond that, in addition, lies a rich field of information concerning the personal thoughts and experiences that form the invisible background of each picture and that are woven into its making. Bill has generously shared some of these ideas and views through personal discussions and interviews with Lloyd Averill and myself as we prepared our respective sections of this book: Averill's informative chronology and bibliography, outlining Bill Holm's event-filled and highly productive life; and my behind-the-scenes overview, combining many personal recollections with an examination of individual paintings, and positioning Holm, the man and the scholar, in terms of his development as a fine artist.

We hope that those of you who see Bill Holm's paintings in this new venue will enjoy not only the pictures themselves but also the subtle cultural realms and historical contexts that he has brought to light. Many individuals have been touched by this man's spirit and energy and by the broad vision that he brings to his life and work, and many of us owe the discovery of the interests that led to our avocations or our professional careers to his example. To many of us, it seems fitting and right to say here: We thank you,

10 / A hunter of the northern Plains, using the ramrod to support his Leman rifle, beads down on a standing antelope. Sent to Allen Chronister. November 1984. Watercolor

11 / A Plateau woman swings a quirt to encourage her horse in pulling a travois load. Sent to Mark Miller. n.d. Watercolor

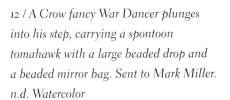

12 / A Crow fancy War Dancer plunges into his step, carrying a spontoon tomahawk with a large beaded drop and a beaded mirror bag. Sent to Mark Miller. n.d. Watercolor

Bill, for your humble and seemingly tireless manner of expressing your love of life and humanity!

It is the paintings themselves, of course, that are the book's strong heart and center. Readers of this volume will feel their own responses to the nature of this artist's work and life, and to the rich legacy of historical information about First Peoples' art and culture that he has painted in these remarkable canvases.

T HE YEARS 1955 AND 1957 SAW THE CREATION OF THE FIRST TWO paintings included in this survey: *Nez Perce Scout* (plate 1), and *Crow Trailing Horses* (plate 2). These horse-centered pictures were purchased by the publishers of *The Western Horseman* magazine, and each was used as a cover illustration during the respective year. The paintings have since been displayed in the publishers' corporate offices, through at least the late 1980s. In composing these paintings, Holm employed the kind of visual framing of the images that he has used in many later canvases, almost as a signature style. Holm's sense of composition is one that brings the viewer close to the subject, inviting the beholder into the picture. Certain other recurring aspects of Holm's entire body of work also appear in these pictures—the richness and accuracy of cultural information, the intimacy of the viewer's contact with the captured moment. But these are only tentative precursors to his future work. Holm himself sees these paintings as exploratory, executed with many outside influences. The details of each of these scenes are rendered in what he has called his "post-University of Washington [art school] style." He notes the impressionistic, rather than documentary, stylization of the plant life, the clouds, and the mountain range, the patterning of color and form, and the overall "designed" quality of both of these renditions. His hallmark sense of historical verity though, is clearly present. It is seen in the appropriate choice of horse breeds, the details of dress and visage of the two men (the face painting, hair style, and ornamentation), and the selection of weapons that each carries. The 1873 Springfield carbine, an early breechloader firing a 45–70 Government cartridge, was the standard U.S. Army cavalry weapon of its day, and one of the most likely rifles to have been acquired by Nez Perce warriors in the frequent skirmishes with the army that marked their flight toward Canada in 1877. At the time of this painting, Holm had an 1873 Springfield in his collection from which to model the rifle held by the Nez Perce scout, but he relied on photos for the details of the 1866 Winchester "Yellow Boy," the lever-action carbine with a brass receiver held by the Crow tracker. He later was able to acquire a fine example of one of these rifles which is now part of his study collection of historic firearms.

14

13 / *A Crow man rides out on a winter hunt, wearing a Hudson's Bay wool capote and a bowcase-quiver slung on his shoulders. Sent to Richard Pohrt. 1986. Watercolor*

14 / *Three Crow-style tipis stand in the serenity of a small encampment. Sent to Mark Miller. January 1987. Graphite*

At this time, Holm had not yet carved and constructed his life-size flexible model (nicknamed "SuperKen") to sit for these pictures, so he himself donned a blanket capote made by his wife Marty and posed for a photograph of the scout. The horse carrying the Crow war raider was modeled on "Gray Lady," one of the horses in the Henderson Camps herd at the time.

In the summer of 1958, having long been intrigued by the beauty and utility of the traditional Northwest Coast canoe forms, Holm set out on the beach of the Henderson Camps to carve a northern-style dugout canoe. He had studied the account of the traditional carving process recorded by George Hunt, the Tlingit/Scottish ethnographer of the Kwakwaka'wakw at the turn of the century.[1] This account outlines and illustrates the series of steps undertaken by the Kwakwaka'wakw canoe builders who were Hunt's informants. Essentially following these plans, and using only nineteenth-century-style hand tools, Holm worked for six weeks, carving the canoe from a twenty-four-foot redcedar log of about thirty inches average diameter. The shaping and hollowing processes reduced 1,000 board feet of log (approximately 4,000 pounds) into a canoe hull that averages one inch in thickness and weighs about ninety-five pounds when bone dry (a 39-to-1 reduction in volume and weight). The canoe has remained in the annual use of the Henderson Camps/Camp Nor'wester staff and campers ever since, carrying four or five paddlers at a time around the islands and beaches of the San Juan archipelago.

Holm recorded the making of this canoe in pictures and a journal, which became the basis of his article "Carving a Kwakiutl Canoe," published in *The Beaver: Magazine of the North* (1961). In the article, he quoted extensively from the George Hunt canoe-making account, creating a bridge to the past and acknowledging the precedence of Hunt's important work. To illustrate the article, he painted *Kwakiutl Canoes* (plate 3), in oil on canvas-board. The vessels in this painting are six to eight feet longer than the one he had carved in 1958, but they are nonetheless based on the intimate experiences with the lines and curves of the hull forms he had gained during the process of carving his canoe, in addition to his study of historic photographs and surviving canoes in the archives and museological institutions of the Northwest. Holm posed for photographs as the model for each paddler, concerned always that each aspect of the scene should appear appropriate and correct.

For anyone who marvels at the beautiful lines and exquisitely designed forms of the canoes of the Northwest Coast, the ones in this picture are a fine and satisfying treat. As seemingly simple and as regular as these lines and forms are from one old traditional canoe to another, it is amazing how easy it is even for skilled artists to miss the true characteristics of their subtle curves, flares, and hollows. Many otherwise fine paintings by talented artists have been flawed by the sometimes stiff, or inaccurate, or just plain ridiculously fanciful depiction of Northwest Coast canoes. Some painters are not familiar enough with the traditional shapes, rendering the canoe's bow and stern forms as they *think* they might have looked, instead of how they actually were or are. This is not, in fact, limited to the mistakes of artists from outside of the Northwest Coast tradition. These vessels are a kind of microcosm unto themselves, though their sensual, efficient lines and swaling forms are embedded in so many other Northwest Coast archetypes, from the obvious bowls and ladles to the more subtle, harmonizing lines of two-dimensional paintings.

In contrast, the old canoe builders of each Northwest Coast culture seem never to have strayed from the fine, traditional lines of the styles of canoes that were indigenous to their areas. It is astonishing, in fact, and emphasizes the internal strength of the old master-apprentice traditions, to look at the dozens and dozens of essentially unvarying canoe forms to be seen in historic photographs, many or even all made by different individual builders, each capturing with seeming ease the subtle forms and relationships that are so often missed by artists and carvers of today. Holm's knack (if such prodigious talent can be fairly characterized as such) for seeing and capturing these fine lines is a natural part of his deeply felt admiration and respect for the ancient ones who devised and developed the designs of these intriguing and efficient vessels. He would simply not feel properly respectful were he to treat these forms lightly or inaccurately, and it is this general motivation that drives his experiential inquiries into his subjects. To carve and refine these shapes, to alter the hull by steaming and bending, to add on the traditionally separate parts of different canoe styles, to repair the inevitable cracks and wear, and to paint the final designs on the fair, smooth hull is to be able to know these vessels intimately, as the living treasures that they are, from the inside out. It is this familiarity and admiration that, at least in part, comes through in the viewpoint that Holm establishes for his viewers. He gives us the benefit of his intimate experiences and brings us in closer, to share the love of fine detail and exquisite form that is part of his own artistic foundation and spirit. This aspect of his work applies to many different kinds of pieces in addition to the canoes, of course, and includes the masks, totem poles, headgear, bead and quill work, and other examples. Many of Holm's carving projects over the years have been, in effect, studies for paintings completed sooner or later. In each case, the hands-on experience of making the objects has translated smoothly into a different sense of intimacy and detail in his paintings than most artists in this field project, helping to make the viewing of his paintings a uniquely rewarding experience.

The painting on the outside of the foreground vessel in *Kwakiutl Canoes* represents the mythical being of Kwakwaka'wakw tradition known as the *Sisiutl* (sée-see-oo<u>hl</u>), a multi-headed, invincible serpent monster that can fly, swim, and burrow in the ground. Pioneer photographer Edward S. Curtis had immortalized a fifty-foot Kwakwaka'wakw canoe with a Sisiutl painted on its sides in his major lifework, *The North American Indian* (1914, vol. 10, p. 15, "A Fair Breeze").[2] Though the structure of that Sisiutl is quite different in style and detail from Holm's, it seems to have offered inspiration for the image in this painting. Holm's version of the Sisiutl, not a direct copy of any known traditional painting, shows his own understanding of the essence of the Kwakwaka'wakw tradition. It exhibits his unique handling of individual shapes and junctures, and, while not relying heavily on the individual stylings of any particular Kwakwaka'wakw artist of the past, can be seen as a synthesis of many styles of the period.

The Sisiutl of Holm's painting is handled in a late-nineteenth-century Kwakwaka'-wakw style, with a black, red, and blue serpent and a white-painted background on the smooth black of the canoe hull (the Sisiutl in the Curtis photo is painted in a simpler white-on-black). The painted features of the Sisiutl reflect the particularly Kwakwaka'-wakw developments of the Northwest Coast two-dimensional traditions. This can be seen as a kind of evolutionary blending of southern coastal historic traditions (as are seen among the Central Coast Salish peoples) and the radically evolved and highly conventionalized styles of the northern Northwest Coast First Nations. In 1957, Holm had written the essential manuscript for his important first book, *Analysis of Form* (1965), as part of his completion of requirements for his teaching certificate at the University of Washington under Dr. Erna Gunther. He had been doing work in the Kwakwaka'wakw and other Northwest Coast styles, for the benefit of the Henderson Camps and other programs, since at least the early 1940s, and the painting on this canoe clearly displays his familiarity and experience with the form.

In addition to the active drama of the *Kwakiutl Canoes* slicing through the rolling green waves, propelled by the focused exertions of the paddlers, so too the towering peaks that frame the location and dwarf the vessels in this picture bring their own sense of powerful, quiet drama. Not situated in some imaginary landscape, the scene is set in the truly spectacular waters of "Kingcome Inlet near the mouth of Wakeman Sound, sometime in the mid-nineteenth century." Holm had photographed this precise location on a kayak trip with his wife Marty some years before. Both were impressed by the grandly majestic quality of the fjord-like, narrow inlet and the near-vertical shorelines of the area, especially as viewed from the water-level seat of their comparatively tiny kayak, a folding Klepper.

The Hudson's Bay Company blanket wrapped about the waist of the forward paddler was designed to pique the interest of the HBC executives who published the magazine, and evidently the bait worked. The painting was used as the cover of the summer

1961 issue of *The Beaver*, as well as in two other canoe-related publications or articles in 1983 and 1984. (Holm gave the original canvas to his lifelong friend and summer camp associate Donn Charnley, who has shared many adventures and experiences with Bill and his family over the years.)

In 1968, ten years after the first canoe, Holm would carve another redcedar dugout, this one thirty-five feet in length and five feet in width. Designed after the Haida ceremonial type, which is deeper and slightly different in detail, this project produced a much larger vessel that required 3,000 board feet of log, but still took a mere six weeks to carve and launch. Holm's straight-ahead, efficient, and unflagging approach to carving makes him capable of completing a project within an amazingly short time frame. (For example, working from old photographs, he completely replicated a thirty-four-foot, Haida-style totem pole for the Burke Museum collection in 1969. The unpainted pole, a masterfully exact copy of the original, was created in just twenty-two non-consecutive days of actual carving.) Launching a thirty-five-foot canoe in six weeks of mostly solo work is nothing short of astonishing. The amount of wood carved away in making a canoe is many times that involved in carving a totem pole! Working with minimal assistance from members of the camp staff that summer, Holm also occasionally employed a small chainsaw on this canoe, a more aggressive tool than he had used on the 1958 vessel. He later remarked that the power saw had enabled him to carve a canoe of at least three times the volume in the same amount of time as one for which only an axe, adzes, and other traditional hand tools were employed. Always the experimenter, always the gatherer of information, Holm has since shared the experiences of making these two canoes, as well as the canoes themselves, with anyone who expressed an interest and enthusiasm for the undertaking. Two generations of Nor'wester staff and campers have paddled both canoes, journeying through many, many nautical miles of San Juan Islands waterways. Several other groups as well have had the pleasure of using the canoes through fundraising auctions and guest paddling trips, and some of the emerging Native canoe makers in this area have called on Holm's knowledge and experience in the making of these vessels.

Restoration Point, at the southern end of Bainbridge Island, Washington, is the setting for a thirty-foot-long canvas painted as a wall mural for the library of Lincoln High School, a Seattle public school in the Wallingford district where Holm received his secondary education and later served on the art faculty. The painting is titled *Vancouver's Ship* Discovery *At Restoration Point, May 1792* (plate 4). With his usual concern for accuracy, Holm photographed the actual location for the scene, with the Olympic mountains silhouetted as they are in the background of the painting. The canoes in this picture represent two distinct types used for centuries in the Puget Sound region: the Nuu-chah-nulth (or Nootkan, or Chinook) type in the foreground, with its characteristically abstract snout at the bow extension; and the indigenous Coast Salish type in the near background, known in the Native Lushootseed (Puget Salish) language as s'tiwátl. Ever the historian, Holm depicts the particularly eighteenth-century stylings of these two canoe types, showing them thinner and less upswept at the bows than their late-nineteenth-century counterparts. Vancouver's vessel, in the distance, was rendered from early drawings of the structure and rigging of the Discovery. The Discovery and the Chatham, along with their lighter craft, were the first European ships to explore and chart the inner waters of Puget Sound.

This extra-long canvas was painted in the Lincoln High School art room, some distance from the library. Holm designed the stretcher for the canvas with a pivoting hinge in the center, so that it could be bent to accommodate the turns and space limitations of the school hallways en route to the painting's final site on the library wall.[3]

Though the size, architectural styles, and real-estate values of the houses on the Restoration Point headlands in this picture have changed considerably in the intervening two centuries, many other aspects of this scene have altered but little. Today these types of canoes can once again be seen paddling these waters, as First Nations in the region work to retrieve the experiences of making and voyaging in the old-style vessels. Such canoes were rarely seen on Puget Sound for decades prior to and following the painting of this scene, but events like the Paddle to Seattle in 1989 and the Full Circle Journeys of the 1990s have reinstated the traditional canoe as a welcome sight in these waters. Holm served as an adviser and consultant on the carving of one of the most faithful recreations of this type; a thirty-five-foot (Nuu-chah-nulth-style) canoe carved by Jerry Jones and Joe Gobin of the Tulalip Tribes in 1988/89 for the Paddle to Seattle.

These early paintings, though few and far between, set the stage for the volume of work that was to come from Bill Holm in the late 1980s and 1990s. In this trio of works, we can see the development of one of the most significant aspects of the Holm style: the *viewpoint* of the picture, the engaging position of the artist's, and by extension, the viewer's eye. As the audience, we are drawn into the picture by the compositions themselves, by the nearness of the artist to his work and his subjects. We do not feel as though we are looking at a scene from some arbitrary, remote distance—we are almost a part of it. We see the Crow tracker as if we are crouched there with him, surveying the trail of the horses he seeks. The Kwakiutl canoe looks as it would from an adjacent vessel. The subject canoe is coming at us, not in a threatening way, but reaching close to deliver some of its message by firsthand contact. This concept is developed even more deliberately in some of the later pictures, but here, in the advance guard of what was to come, the uniqueness of Holm's relationship to his work shines through, providing an experience for the viewer that is carefully conceived, honed with familiarity and accuracy, and polished with his love of light, color, and form.

In 1984 Holm completed carving the thirty-five-foot cedar frontal pole for the exterior wall of his studio north of Seattle, and a day was set aside for raising the pole into place. He designed two special projects for this event, to which a large number of friends and colleagues had been invited. One was an experimental system of mounting and raising the pole, utilizing a concrete base/counterweight that was poured in the horizontal position, already attached to a strongback mounted in the hollowed rear of the pole. The second project was the creation of a limited-edition serigraph (plate 5), to be given out like a potlatch gift to those in attendance at the pole raising.

Rather than raise the newly carved pole onto a concrete base poured at ground level, Holm decided to incorporate such a base onto the lower end of the pole as a counterweight. The idea worked out beautifully as planned. The shape of the base/counterweight was formed up and the concrete poured, in the place of the traditional lower section of the pole that would be buried in the ground. This attached weight would assist in raising the upper end of the pole in the critical first few feet of elevation angle, by levering down on the opposite side of a steel-pipe fulcrum braced at the edge of the hole dug for the concrete base. (The fulcrum was placed against a blank spot on the front of the pole, onto which the carved face of a subsidiary figure was fastened afterward. This face also covered the bolts that fastened the pole to the strongback.) The pole was laid face down and was going to be pulled up with its back against the front of the studio wall. There was no place above and behind the studio for ropes to be led with which to raise it up, and space was quite limited in front of the studio as well. Therefore, a cable and winch were used in place of the usual arrangement of two ropes led out at angles from the top of a pole being raised. The steel cable was attached to a rope bound near the top of the pole, and led to a pulley block tied up in a tree behind the studio. This in turn led the cable back, forward of the house, to where a heavy manual winch was fastened to a tree. Cranking on the winch would then pull the top of the pole into its place above the gable of the studio roof.

Except for a short hitch, caused by a slightly too-low purchase angle on the pulley in the tree, the raising of the pole went smoothly. When the wooden braces holding up the counterweight were removed, the concrete base tipped down into the hole beneath it. This raised the top of the pole on the opposite side of the fulcrum to nearly enough of an angle for the cable to continue raising it the rest of the way. But tightening up on the winch cable was not yet enough to budge the top of the pole. A small hand-power boost by volunteers added the necessary one or two feet of additional angle, and the winch then eased the pole up into position to the triumphant cheers of the crowd. The back-filling of the hole around the concrete base supported the frontal pole in its vertical position.

The serigraph Holm produced for the event was less experimental than the pole-raising technique, but it nonetheless required a number of steps in the progress of its creation. Seven separate colors were used in the printing process, and each color printing was done using the same screen. Beginning with the lightest colors, the white and nearly white highlights, Holm essentially painted the picture right on the silk screen. He successively masked off those areas where each previously printed color was to remain, working with a water-based compound over a pencil drawing of the picture's image. The darkest layers of ink were the last to be masked off and printed through the screen. Since there was no painted color original from which the individual copies were printed, and the shape of each color area was "painted" directly on the screen, each print is like an original of the image. The Holms use variations of this printing technique to produce very special Christmas cards, for which Bill creates a new image every year.

Following his formal retirement in 1985 from the curatorial and professional aspects of his career, Holm was able to focus more intensively on his painting. He moved into a period of far more prolific production than the previous decades had allowed. In 1986, he was one of several art-history professionals invited by Peter Corey of the Sheldon Jackson Museum in Sitka, Alaska, to contribute a scholarly article to an illustrated catalog of the Sheldon Jackson Museum collection, the oldest in that state and one with prominent national recognition. The catalog, *Faces, Voices, and Dreams* (Corey, ed., 1987), was published in honor of the one-hundredth anniversary of the institution in 1988.[4]

Holm's article, "The Head canoe" (143–55), focused on the history and development of many of the traditional canoe types in use on the Northwest Coast in the eighteenth and nineteenth centuries. The archaic style of vessel known as the head canoe has long intrigued and interested Holm. A graphically unique vessel-form, the head canoe was completely eclipsed over a span of time in the early nineteenth century by what is generally called the northern canoe type, the style he had replicated in 1958 and 1968. (Holm carved his third traditional canoe in 1978. This was an eleven-foot-long Nuu-chah-nulth type made as a part-time dinghy for his 27-foot sailboat.) The article demonstrates the relationship of the head canoe form to that of the smaller and more commonly utilitarian *spruce canoe* (*séet yakw* in Tlingit, named for the trees from which they were often traditionally made), a vessel type that continued to be made well into the twentieth century in northern Southeast Alaska. The article also describes and illustrates some aspects of the transition from the head canoe to the northern type, using drawings done by Holm, plus a couple of very unusual paintings of these vessels executed by an early nineteenth-century Tlingit artist on the inside of a bent-corner food dish of the period (154, figs. 11, 12).

With his ongoing enthusiasm for the canoe forms and his new-found freedom from former time constraints, Holm seized the opportunity to combine the images of all three of these canoe types in a single picture: *Potlatch Guests Arriving at Sitka, Winter 1803* (plate 6). This painting was reproduced in a two-page spread for the catalog *Faces, Voices, and Dreams* (148–49), as well as in poster form for distribution by the Friends of the Sheldon Jackson Museum. (This group is considering a possible reprinting.) The original painting is part of the collection of the Alaska State Museums.[5]

A fairly large canvas, this picture is a marvel of historic recreation as well as a grand illustration of Bill Holm's skills as a documentarian and a visionary artist. He sets the scene with the beachfront of the *Shee-atiká* (Sitka) village in the immediate foreground (a site today crowded with the homes, businesses, and fish-processing plants of Katlian Street in downtown Sitka, as well as a handful of remaining Tlingit clan houses of early-twentieth-century vintage). Across the narrow channel is the shore of Japonski Island, named by the Russians to honor the survivors of the wreck (in 1805) of an early-nineteenth-century Japanese merchant ship that had drifted to the area along the trans-Pacific Japanese Current (known in Japan as the *Kuroshio*).[6] The lofty, symmetrical cone of the dormant volcano named Mt. Edgecumbe appears over the Japonski Island forest. In the channel, four large canoes filled with clan members invited from other Tlingit villages have assembled for a ritual approach to the beach, during which songs, dances, and oratory are shared as a prelude to coming ashore for a potlatch (a ceremonial gathering known as *Koo.éex* in the Tlingit language). Two performers in peace-dance regalia are in action in the bows of two of the head canoes in the picture, while the crew members boom out the rhythm of the accompanying song on the gunwales of the canoes with the ends of their paddles. Another large head canoe and one of the early northern type drift quietly alongside, steadied by a few of the paddlers while their clan leaders stand in respect for the occasion. Early-morning sunlight from the low southeast highlights the surfaces of the canoe hulls and the traditional formline paintings that embellish them.

In the foreground, the bows of three of the smaller spruce canoes can be seen in their usual kind of storage locations along the high tideline. One of these is covered by a yellowcedar-bark mat to shield it from the drying and cracking influences of direct sunlight; another holds a pair of paddles, and we can see what may be the handle of a herring rake, an ingenious canoe-borne implement employed in the harvest of food and roe herring from the massive shoals of these fish that once swarmed into Sitka Sound by the millions to spawn in the early springtime. (A much-reduced population of herring still returns to Sitka Sound and other Southeast Alaska locations in late March, to become the target of a massive and high-tech assault from a small number of limited-entry seine boats of the commercial fishing industry.) A clan leader of the Sitka tribes stands on the beach, poised in welcome, dressed in regalia appropriate for the place and time period.

The most studious critique of this picture would find nothing that was not carefully considered for its appropriateness to the scene: the canoes themselves, the regalia, the trees of the forest. The presence of each is the result of Holm's experience with these materials over his long academic career and decades of personal interest and study. The unusual shape of the paddle tips in use in this picture differs from that of the typical Tlingit paddle preserved in museums or visible in nineteenth-century photographs of this area, and is modeled after an archaic form that sometimes accompanies very old Native-made models of head canoes that are found in museums around the globe. The same shape of paddle blade appears in the Tlingit painting of canoes, inside the food dish illustrated in *Faces, Voices, and Dreams* (154).

In order to render accurately the views and perspective relationships of the canoes in the picture, Holm employed his ingenuity in model making and slide projection. He adapted a previously made model of a small northern-style canoe, modifying one end into the shape of a spruce canoe (which as a group were nearly identical on bow and stern), and posing it in the various positions seen among the canoes in the near foreground of the finished painting. To properly represent the head canoes at different angles, as well as the foreshortening apparent in the painted designs on their hulls, he taped together matboard cutouts into a simplified but accurately shaped head-canoe model with all the curves and flares of the originals. The ends of this model canoe were painted white, and onto this surface he projected 35 mm slides of the paintings found on certain historic canoe models, which he had photographed in various museums. By shining the correctly scaled images of these paintings straight onto the side of the matboard model, and by rotating this arrangement to the appropriate angle for each canoe in the Sitka painting, he was able to replicate even the most radical foreshortening of the canoe hulls and painted designs with considerable ease.

Holm had used the conceptual reverse of this slide-projection process at least once before. In that case, the challenge was to see the fine formline painting on the side of a particular nineteenth-century chest that he had photographed some years before in the Field Museum of Natural History in Chicago. The photographic record he had was limited to one view, taken slightly off to the side, that focused primarily on the design on the front of the chest. The side painting was at an extreme angle and greatly foreshortened,

24

which made it difficult to see and adequately interpret the painted design. Working with his black-and-white negative of the chest picture, Holm mounted the film in a photographic enlarger in the usual way, but he tilted the table on which the printing paper was to be exposed as close as possible to the angle of foreshortening that existed in the side of the chest in the photo. When the resulting print was developed, the image on it appeared almost as if it had been photographed straight on! Today, of course, such manipulations are routinely done with the assistance of computers and scanners and swillions of bytes of digital memory. In the early 1970s, however, such technology was not available to the average household, and a more inventive solution to this kind of problem had to be imagined.

Other pieces of the Sitka canoe scene were based on actual artifacts that survive from the period represented in the picture. The semi-conical hat with five woven rings and two especially long ermine-skins was based on an example collected at Sitka by George Emmons, now housed in the Field Museum, Chicago (53024-1). Some pieces of Tlingit origin, now in the collection of Bill and Marty Holm, appear in this picture: the staff held by the clan leader in the foreground, and the frontlet worn by the peace dancer in the second canoe from the left. The box drum tilted in use in the center of the third canoe from the left is based on one that Holm made in the middle 1960s. Assembled from laminated boards (not in bent-corner style), the box drum has seen thirty years of use in the big-house on Lopez Island during camp sessions, and at performances of all kinds by many different groups to whom Holm has generously loaned the drum for the enhancement of singing and dancing in the traditional style.

The woven robe on the chieftain in the foreground and the others visible at a distance in the canoes are based on the small number of very early, geometrically decorated examples of this type which have survived in the world's museums. As noted in the caption for this picture, this type of weaving was the prevalent technique in the generations prior to the onset of Euro-American contact in the region in the late eighteenth century. Known today as the "Raven's Tail" technique (Samuel 1987), this style of work was supplanted by the weaving of curvilinear designs in the style known today as "Chilkat" weaving. In order to depict properly the drapery and perspective of this type of robe in use, Holm painted the designs on a piece of old tipi canvas and draped it over the shoulders of SuperKen, his newly created wooden model. Bill ingeniously carved this full-size person of redcedar, assembling the shoulders, elbows, wrists, fingers, and other joints with hinge pins and elastic cord, like the small, flexible, wooden artist's mannequins available commercially. Unlike the little commercial mannequins, however, SuperKen's face is naturalistically carved, using Native American features of a general type. His uncannily realistic appearance has seriously startled more than one visitor to Holm's studio, where he sits or stands motionless in some corner of the room, dressed in cotton shirt, pants, and a cap (when not decked out in articles of traditional regalia for a picture).

Also painted in 1987, *Spring Hunt* (plate 7) brings us back to the plateau region east of the Cascade Mountains, near the big bend in the Columbia River in what is today the territory of the Yakama Confederated Tribes. Holm planned this picture in 1977, while traveling about the country photographing Northwest Coast and other artifacts during a research sabbatical from the Burke Museum. He speaks of being fascinated by watching the aerial antics of magpies in the interior plateau region, and he sketched this painting on the back of a business card during a meal stop on the road (fig. 15). The foreground originally was designed to include a swooping magpie, and Holm went so far as to photocopy a magpie's wing from the natural history collection at the Burke as a model for the bird in the painting. As he worked on the actual painting (ten years later), however, he deleted the image of the magpie, finding it distracting within the rest of the composition. The resulting open space in this picture is one of its strongest points, lending an immediate sense of the quiet expanse of territory in the domain of the hunter. The low winter light and shadows further lend a special, magical quality to the scene.

Dressed in a wool capote, sewn from a Hudson's Bay Company blanket, the hunter rests his percussion rifle across his lap. This was a common trade gun of a type made by Henry Leman of Philadelphia. Holm owns a similar trade-era rifle, though not a Leman, which was a well-known gun in the period and time of the picture. He based the rifle in the scene on the gun he had, with modifications to reflect the detailings of the Leman manufacture. Posing SuperKen as seated on a horse (fig. 16), wearing Marty's capote (the same garment as seen in plates 15 and 26), he also included an elk antler quirt that he had made in the Plateau style, and an old powder horn from his own collection. When his friend Dave Munsell saw the painting in progress, he asked, "Where's his bullet pouch?" So Holm painted one in.

Though the landscape in this image is imaginary rather than specific, Holm referenced the appearance of eastern Washington sagebrush with actual photographs and planned the lighting of a winter's morning by illuminating SuperKen with lamps in his studio. The move toward a more documentary style in the full rendering of this scene is especially apparent when compared with the similar settings of *Nez Perce Scout* (plate 1) and *Crow Trailing Horses* (plate 2). Here, the light, wispy clouds have a very natural quality when contrasted with the more impressionistic influences and movements of the sky patterns in the paintings from twenty years earlier.

For the centennial celebration of the Burke Museum in 1989, Robin Wright (successor to Holm's curatorial position there) and the director and staff of the museum mounted

15 / *Original sketch for* Spring Hunt *(plate 7), done on the back of a business card. 1977. Graphite.*

16 / *SuperKen rides his "pony" in the studio, dressed as a Plateau hunter for* Spring Hunt *(plate 7).*

a landmark exhibition—*A Time of Gathering: Native Heritage in Washington State* (ATOG). The exhibition brought together the Native traditions from east and west of the Cascade Mountains, and Native leaders were involved throughout the many months of preparation. Bill Holm composed two images to reflect the content and spirit of the undertaking, *Going Visiting* (plate 8), and *Parade* (plate 9). *Going Visiting* was used as a promotional poster for the Burke Museum's Northwest Coast Canoes exhibit, and *Parade* was later reproduced as a limited edition print. The planning period for the ATOG show coincided with another of Holm's undertakings. He was working with the Tulalip carvers to replicate the fine, old Nuu-chah-nulth-style canoe that had survived on the reservation in the collection of the Chief Shelton family, and he projected some of his enthusiasm for that project into the painting of *Going Visiting*. Photographs taken by Holm in 1973 of the thirty-five-foot Shelton canoe served to inspire both projects, and the beautiful, delicate lines of that treasured old vessel were successfully transferred to each new venue. The canoe in this painting exhibits the greater upsweep of the bow form that is typical of later historic period Nuu-chah-nulth-style canoes, like the Shelton vessel, in contrast to the lower, straighter lines of the eighteenth-century canoes, such as the one located off Restoration Point in the 1966 painting (plate 4). Also shown here are the two circular, eyelike piercings on the bow extension, which some First Peoples say identifies a freight or traveling canoe.

Holm chose to represent the canoe travelers of this painting in the typical daily dress of Puget Sound First Peoples in the late nineteenth century: Euro-American-style clothing, wool blankets, and in one case, a Coast Salish-style cedar-bark hat. When someone questioned the depiction of western-style garments, rather than traditional Native clothing, Robin Wright replied: "We're in the business of education, after all." Holm's sense of historical reality for any scene includes the proper appearance for the particular time and place, and Puget Sound in 1889 had seen a huge influx of settlers and developers since the establishment of the first Euro-American pioneer community on Alki Point in 1854. Studio and field photographs of First Peoples from this period also served as the inspiration for the kinds of dress in common use at that time.

Other "research" added to the spirit and life of this painting: In order to help capture the moment, Holm photographed the rolling and cresting of Puget Sound waves from his family's small sailboat and from the shore at Goose Point, their property on the south end of Lopez Island. There, on one great, stormy winter day, exactly the setting Holm was striving for in this image, he rigged up a quick set of sails near the open, windswept point. Using a tipi pole for a mast, an old tipi canvas for the sail, and a split, shaped, and smoothed light spar for the diagonal sprit of the sail rig, he was able to photograph the same types of light and sky conditions that were to play upon the sails of the big traveling-canoe in the picture. In addition, his own experiences of sailing the 1968 Haida-style canoe around the area had given him knowledge of the canoe's actions and capabilities under sail and provided him with the very real physical thrill that is captured in the attitude of the man riding the bow of the canoe in this painting.[7]

The second of the ATOG-inspired paintings depicts a Plateau couple in their heirloom finery taking part in a mounted celebration. *Parade* (plate 9) is a full and visually rich painting, yet nothing appears in the picture by chance. The materials, the construction and decoration of the various objects, the styles of designs employed — all reflect the experience and knowledge of the painter and illustrate the joy he feels in being able to assemble and compose these individually rare and obscure objects into complete images, images that recall and celebrate the glory and level of ingenuity attained by the First Peoples of the past.

Such a scene is *Parade*, which, along with *Raven Warrior* (plate 17), made up the first two Bill Holm paintings to be reproduced as limited-edition prints for sale to a wider audience. The apparently industrious couple in this view is decked out in the way that perhaps many were in that century-old period, and their composite image has been brought forward to our time and place. Today, of course, First Peoples in this region still dress in similar finery, and have been immortalized by a plethora of contemporary photographers in rich, sharp color for display in books, magazines, and calendars. But, as beautiful and inspiring as the modern outfits of the pow-wow culture are, only a precious few of the original ancestor outfits or articles are also there, still to be seen and worn and recognized for their antiquity and longevity. In *Parade*, generations of effort are represented in the design, preparation, and execution of the fine work that is immortalized in this scene. Fortunately, the skill and knowledge of the contemporary artist are able to reconstitute the many glimmering pieces of this historic puzzle for us to admire and appreciate today, just as it surely was in its own day.

Holm made the preliminary sketch for this picture in Juneau, Alaska, on a restaurant place mat, in a spare moment. The images of the many different traditional pieces that he has assembled in the final picture originated both from actual historic objects and from the artist's imagination, based on the appropriate styles of similar objects known from his research and study. The woman's fine dress is based on an old Plateau piece in the Holm collection, though the seed beads on the yoke of that garment have been transmuted for this picture into "pony" beads, an early material more typical of Plateau garments from the first half of the nineteenth century. The seed-beaded designs on the sleeve strips of the painted dress, however, are the same as on the original garment of mountain sheep skin. The woven hat, a style unique among Plateau First

Nations, is directly based on a hat in the Holm collection, as are the beaded leggings of the woman. Other decorated pieces in the picture are composites based on the styles of known objects of the type, such as the blanket strip on the woman's lap, the man's shirt, the martingale on the woman's horse and the covering "mask" on the man's,[8] the stirrups of the woman's saddle, the parfleche case, and the upright feather warbonnet of the male rider. As in all of Holm's paintings, the feathers of this bonnet, the coup stick, and the downlike, fluffy feather on the woman's hat are all based directly on actual feathers in his collection, acquired prior to the 1962 legislative restrictions on the ownership of eagle parts. Out of respect for their individual uniqueness and magical beauty, he is simply not satisfied to paint generic feather forms. He always models real feathers of the appropriate type for each of their appearances. Because he is painting for his friends, associates, and a wide range of knowledgeable people who make up his primary audience, Holm wants everything to "look right," from beads and patterns to feathers and skin textures. He wants to represent accurately the play of light on the various surfaces, the colors, textures, forms, and designs of the traditional pieces, as they truly appear to those who are most familiar with them.

*Beach Harvest, Puget Sound* (plate 10) depicts what must have been an almost daily occurrence of many of the broad, flat beaches of this protected inland waterway. Clams and cockles were gathered in abundance to be steamed and eaten fresh, or shucked and braided together on sticks for smoking and drying to preserve them for future consumption or trade. The tons of pulverized shells that have accumulated in the massive middens that mark the sites used for seasonal camps and villages on the Northwest Coast attest to the importance of bivalves in the First Peoples' traditional diet. Bill and Marty Holm frequently walk on Richmond Beach near their Seattle home. Richmond Beach is part of a beach and foreshore ecosystem, extending north to the city of Edmonds, which once saw regular use as a traveling camp and harvesting site by many First Nations in the not-so-distant past. This same area serves as this picture's setting. The headlands of the Kitsap Peninsula and the haze-lightened Olympic Mountains frame the background of the painting, topped by the twin peaks of The Brothers on the left and Mount Constance on the right of the scene.

Preparations for the ATOG exhibit had brought out several small Puget Sound–style canoes from the Burke Museum storage, which may have helped to kindle Holm's interest in this particular type of vessel from within his enduring appreciation of canoes in general. His article on the head canoe for the 1987 *Faces, Voices, and Dreams* catalog had discussed the possible origins of the "northern" canoe type from the parent characteristics of the Coast Salish model, of which the canoe in this picture is a small example.

Unlike the head- and spruce-canoe hull-shapes, on which the end-fins are carved to a thin entry from top to bottom, the ends of the Coast Salish canoe feature a flared-out transition from the thin entry to the much wider breadth of the gunwale shapes. This hollowed flare actually extends along the entire length of the canoe just below the gunwale, and becomes wider and more pronounced as it approaches the tip of the bow and stern. Though neither the bow nor stern is curved upward very high at the ends, this outward flare serves perfectly to turn off waters into which the canoe cuts with its thin stem or stern entries. Made for the sounds and inlets of the Gulf of Georgia and Puget Sound, this type of canoe was documented as far north as the tip of Vancouver Island by the drawings of early explorers. Holm has postulated that the near-vertical cutwater of the bow, the slanting stern line, and the flared gunwales of these canoes served as the inspiration for the historic development of the northern canoe form. The ends of the northern canoe are designed with a dramatic upward curl that raises the flare of the gunwales high enough to accommodate the larger swells and breaking seas of the outer coast north of Vancouver Island and far out to the shores of Haida Gwaii, the Queen Charlotte Islands.

In 1990, Holm carved a thirteen-foot Coast Salish canoe of the type known in Lushootseed as s'*dagwił*, and it is a dead ringer for the one in this quiet, peaceful painting. Interested as ever in the information that such an endeavor could provide to others, he carefully measured and drew the lines of the canoe prior to and after the steaming of the hull and the spreading-out of the gunwale width. These drawings, along with others that he has made of his own canoes and many of the ones in various museum collections, document the details of the hull forms and the steaming dynamic that can be of invaluable use to coming generations of canoe makers. (Holm's projected publication of a "canoe book" that will contain historic information, photographs, drawings, and all of his [and others'] experience in traditional canoes and canoe making, will be a valuable and welcome volume, the culmination of many of his fondest efforts.)

The style of paddle, the cattail mat (to cushion the paddler's knees), and the cedar-bark bailer in the canoe in *Beach Harvest* are typical of those made by Puget Sound First Nations, as is the ingenious and beautiful design of the gathering basket at the clam digger's feet. The open, sievelike weave of these containers allows the sand and mud to be easily rinsed off the clams by dunking the basket in clean water. It also keeps the bearer from carrying any extra, unnecessary water weight, and prevents the possibility of rainwater filling the container on the journey home by canoe or on foot. The woman's simple cedar-bark skirt was a common item of dress in the pre-contact period in which this scene is set, as were the native-copper bracelets and dentalium shell earrings she is wearing. Dentalia were known about the coast as *héixwa*, a term drawn from the

Nuu-chah-nulth language and used in the widespread trade language known as the "Chinook jargon." These rare and difficult-to-harvest shells were collected by the Makah and Nuu-chah-nulth of the outer coast and were traded north, south, and eastward over great distances, with their exchange value increasing in relation to the distance traveled.

Invited to contribute a piece to the second annual Prix Dakota exhibition of the High Plains Heritage Center in Spearfish, South Dakota, Holm produced *Ate He Ye Lo — So Says the Father* (plate 11). The focus of the 1990 exhibition was the centennial of the 1890 massacre by U.S. Army troops and scouts of over two hundred peaceful Lakota at Wounded Knee, South Dakota. Chief Bigfoot's band of Minneconjou Lakota, mostly elders, women, and children, had gathered to hold a Ghost Dance, a ritual of hope and resurrection that had spread like wildfire across the plains in the waning years of the nineteenth century. When they were ordered to assemble near Wounded Knee Creek one cold winter morning to be disarmed by the soldiers, the tension of the moment broke out into spontaneous violence. Nearly all of the Lakota were mown down by the ensuing horrendous crossfire of Hotchkiss breechloading guns and the unrelenting pursuit of mounted soldiers.

Not inclined to deal with the more grisly aspects of the event, such as were recorded after the battle in numerous photographs of the day, Holm elected to represent a scene from the Ghost Dance. Nancy K. George, of Nez Perce and Nooksack heritage, and I posed for pictures that would model the clasped hands of the Ghost Dance circle. Holm then painted some muslin for the dresses and tunic, one at a time using colored chalk, with designs typical of Plains Ghost Dance imagery. SuperKen modeled the variously painted garments in three different sittings for the finished picture. The shield worn on the back of the male dancer in the center of the image comes from the Holm collection, an old original shield from the Rosebud reservation (near the Wounded Knee site) collected around 1910.

So often when Bill Holm gets involved in some research or production effort — a canoe, a Northwest trade gun, or a quilled or beaded piece — his focus and energy for the project spills over into the creation of another painting. His hands are always busy, whether he is waiting in a ferry line, sitting on an airplane, watching a football game, or just puttering about in his studio with various tools and materials. The record of his paintings reads like a running diary of his many creative projects. Two such primary and enduring interests are documented in *Spontoon Tomahawk* (plate 12): the quill-wrapped horsehair technique, and general blacksmithing.

17 / *Detail of Holm's fingers performing the rhythmic motions of the technique of quill-wrapped horsehair embroidery. This piece was made for the transmontane-style quill-wrapped horsehair shirt shown in several of his paintings.*

With his abiding engagement in the processes of bead and quill work, Holm turned his interest at about this time toward the rare and insufficiently documented technique of quill-wrapped horsehair decoration (see fig. 17). He began creating a research example of one of the longish, narrow shirt-strips, which are made up of several lanes of small horse-hair bundles wrapped by porcupine quills and bordered by narrow, beaded edging. Four such beaded and quilled strips combine to decorate the shoulders and sleeves of a rare type of western Plains and Plateau man's shirt, such as the one depicted in *Spontoon Tomahawk*.[9] The first strip he made did not satisfy his sense of quality (though ordinary people were pretty blown away by it!), so he made two new shoulder pieces and two narrower ones for the sleeve strips of a shirt. The shirt was sewn together from antelope skins he had recently cleaned, scraped, and brain-tanned.[10]

At the time this painting was completed, he had finished one of the shoulder strips for the shirt and one of the beaded triangular "bibs" that decorate the neckline on the front and back. From within the painting glows the image of the shirt that existed in his mind's eye and which was coming together stitch by stitch in little segments of his world. The leggings worn by the center figure are similarly based on real subjects. In this case, Holm had one old beaded legging strip in his collection, and he commissioned his friend, expert bead worker Louie Jull, to replicate a mate to it, with which he put together the pair of leggings painted in this picture. The split-horn-type bonnet is based loosely on a similar example housed in the Phoebe Hearst Museum, San Francisco. The moccasins are painted after a pair of pony-beaded examples in the collection of the National Museum of Natural History, Smithsonian Institution, Washington, D.C. The ATOG exhibit at the Burke Museum included a full-scale tule mat lodge, constructed in the traditional manner by James Selam and his family from the Yakama Confederated Tribes. The impression that this lodge made on Holm is acknowledged in the background of the painting. Hung on one of the lodge poles is a parfleche container modeled after one in the Burke Museum's collection, and the blanket strip wrapped about the man seated on tule mats at the rear is painted after an original Plateau-style example in the Holm collection.

The art of blacksmithing is one of Bill Holm's lesser-developed skills, but one that he has employed in making and modifying carving tools for his sculptural work, and has experimented with for the creation of such interesting objects as the type of spontoon tomahawk illustrated in this picture. The particular example shown here is based on one in the Burke Museum, a large piece that had been broken and actually came from two different sites along the Columbia River. It exemplifies a form that holds a special fascination for the artist. Not long after I first got to know Bill (this would have been about 1970), we worked together on one attempt to forge out such a spontoon tomahawk. We were not very successful as it turned out that time, but after a long day of cranking the forge, breathing the inevitable coal smoke, and banging on set hammers and anvils, I realized that I was severely hooked! Before long, I had a hand forge, anvil, and smithing tools of my own that I still occasionally use in the making of special tools for carving and canoe making, all of which are experiences that I first encountered with Bill's introduction.

Another of Holm's long-enduring interests has focused on the particular piece of refined smithing and hand-manufacture known as the Northwest Trade Gun, a style of musket developed by European gunsmiths in response to some particular demands by Native American peoples, based on their historically favorite weapons of the type. Holm has acquired several of these simple, handsome muskets for his study collection, and he has "artifaked" one by modifying the barrel and stock characteristics of a similar period gun into the particular styles of the Northwest Gun. This is a shortened-barrel version, on which he has further relief-carved the stock and fore-end with finely worked Northwest Coast two-dimensional designs that make it quite a head-turner![11]

The wide, panoramic composition of *The Flankers* (plate 13) was originally designed to be a framed background in which the image of a nearly full-size Northwest Trade Gun was to be highlighted. When Holm finished roughing-in the picture, however, he realized (with the help of Marty's objective eye!) that the gun would only clutter it up—so he left it out. The resultant wide expanse of territory surveyed by the two mounted trail guards makes for an inspiring composition and conveys a great deal about Montana and the world of its First Peoples. Holm's fondness for the look, the feel, and the fine wood, brass, and iron details of the Northwest Trade Gun has found expression elsewhere in his paintings. In addition to the guns held in the image of *The Flankers*, one can be seen held at the ready by the *Raven Warrior* (plate 17). Another lies across a man's lap in the foreground of *Purifying the Shield* (plate 14). One is held high by a warrior in *The Taunt* (plate 25), and some are stored in protective coverings, such as those seen in *The Dandies* (plate 16), and the *Blue Beaded Guncase* (plate 28).

ALTHOUGH ANY DATE USED TO MARK A TRANSITION MUST OFTEN be arbitrarily selected, Bill Holm's painting production seems really to have taken off in the decade of the 1990s. Correspondence, consultations, and professional conferences still demand time and energy, but those hours free of other pursuits in this period have more often found him in the shelter of his studio, at work on another visual history on canvas.

One of Holm's favorite and most challenging motivations for the creation of a new painting is to exchange the finished piece for some treasured object owned or made by one of his many friends and colleagues in the field. A clear motive is readily envisioned in the object to be exchanged, and a special challenge lies in the high standards of such an audience. These are people most familiar with and knowledgeable about the types of details that Holm likes to represent and work with in his art. *Purifying the Shield* (plate 14) is one of these creations, commissioned by expert beadworker Mark Miller, who made a spectacular Crow/Plateau–style bandoleer bag in trade for the picture.[12] Miller chose the general subject matter for the picture, but he left the rest up to the artist. Holm sketched the basic idea for the composition on the back of the program from a concert he attended in Denver one evening with Dick Conn of the Denver Art Museum. (One might wonder how much the spirit and energy of the music may have contributed to the final outcome.) He then expanded on this draft of the picture with a charcoal drawing, and sent that to Miller for final approval, which was readily and enthusiastically granted. Miller himself designed the image on the shield in the painting, based as these images typically are on the particular dreams and visions of their owners. Holm naturally included some pieces from his own technical work and family collection. The shirt worn by the pipe carrier in the upper right is based largely on his own quill-wrapped horsehair shirt, then recently completed. The smudge-fire tender on the left wears quill-wrapped horsehair-embellished moccasins modeled on existing pairs (and which inspired Holm to create his own pair using this technique. The pair made by him appears in *The Mountain Lion Skin Quiver* [plate 27]). The parfleche medicine case, tipi lining, flintlock Northwest Gun, split-horn bonnet, and leggings worn by the shield holder are all based on related articles from Crow traditions, while the pipe bag in the right center is based directly on a fine example that appeared in a Sotheby's auction catalog at about this time. (Holm was pleased that Miller recognized the particular bag right away in the finished painting.)

The painting entitled *The Decision* (plate 15) is the full color-embellished version of a pencil drawing executed in 1989. Holm submitted the drawing to the Prix Dakota exhibition at the High Plains Heritage Center that year, at which time the Custer battle was the theme of the exhibition. The battle at the Little Bighorn was always a topic of great interest to Holm, and he recalls drawing the same basic subject while he was a student in junior high school in Seattle, some fifty years earlier. Holm researched the imagery of this picture with particularly studious attention to detail. As are many historians, he was familiar with the essential background of the days leading up to and including the fatal assault on the Lakota/Cheyenne village by the Seventh Calvary on June 25, 1876. But he nonetheless needed to know a great many more seemingly insignificant facts before he would feel pleased with the results of his effort.

He was familiar with pictures of a series of pictographs by White Swan, the Crow Scout, done on muslins and buffalo robes in the years following the fateful encounter. White Swan is shown kneeling with his telescope in Holm's painting. The pictographs revealed a number of interesting details, such as White Swan with a telescope, observing the distant village, and wearing a hat with an eagle feather attached to it. Another showed White Swan with a wool capote made from a Hudson's Bay blanket. Some scholars have questioned whether these images in fact represented the Custer engagement, since that battle took place at the end of June. Various Indian accounts of the encounter, though, mentioned White Swan's and other scouts' capotes. White Swan and the others had lain up on this ridge from midnight to the first light of dawn, trying to identify the location of the village which turned out to be some fifteen miles distant. Snow had, in fact, fallen on the Custer expedition on the first of June, and it had been raining previous to their arrival at this site. Knowledge of such conditions would seem to warrant the inclusion of the extra garment.

Holm's own experience with the area also corroborated certain details of the oral accounts. Traveling through the area en route from an earlier Prix Dakota show in Spearfish, South Dakota, Bill and Marty had stopped and searched for this site in the region of the Little Bighorn Battlefield National Monument. They were there on July first, about a week after the anniversary of the event, and even at that time the mornings were quite chilly. They set out at seven o'clock, bundled up in jackets, and before long they succeeded in locating what was at least the general area of the "Crow's Nest" lookout, as the peak of the ridge in this painting has been called. They stood on the ridge around 9:00 A.M., at the same time of day that Custer had stood there with the scouts. Holm said later that, based on this visit, he would certainly have "been glad to have had a capote" to keep warm in the wee hours before the dawn.

Additional historical accounts provided further details: Custer's uncharacteristically short haircut, obtained by him prior to embarking on this mission; his buckskin jacket in place of regulation uniform; the pairs of binoculars held by Custer and Charley Reynolds, the man at the rear of this group, who also is recorded as having had a badly infected hand. In creating likenesses of the soldiers, Holm consulted their earlier photographs. The images of the Crow scouts Goes Ahead (at the left of the group, behind Custer) and White Swan were based on photographs made in the years after the battle, which both had managed to survive. A photograph by Dr. Joseph K. Dixon, in the conference documentation book by Rodman Wanamaker, entitled "The Vanishing Race," depicts a fairly clear profile of Goes Ahead. This profile has always reminded Holm of his own father (though he's of Swedish, not Crow, heritage), which he says made it especially easy for him to render this face with familiarity. The third Crow scout in this scene, White Man Runs Him, is shown pointing out the site of the distant village encampment to the disbelieving Custer. White Man Runs Him has also been included in historic photographs, and Holm relied on these and on composites of other Crow people of the period for the scout's traditional hair style and physical features.

Holm relates that he first painted the image of Goes Ahead holding a red blanket, for lack of any other specific information. Encountering a copy of an obscure Montana newspaper account by the son-in-law of Goes Ahead, he read that the Crow scout had described being on this particular summit with a white blanket capote and a wolf skin scout-medicine, with a red stripe and red cloth tied about the tail. (The same wolf skin, as it turns out, and a different capote, appear in Edward Curtis's picture taken of the surviving Crow scouts on the battlefield in the early 1900s). Armed with this new information, Holm right away painted over the red blanket with the images of the capote and wolf skin that are now displayed in the painting.

The exploratory trip to the area with Marty also provided photographs of the ridge, its panorama, and its precise appearance: the grasses, trees, and rocks that, like nearly everything in this area, have changed remarkably little in the intervening one hundred and twenty-plus years since this tragic and historic event transpired.

In contrast to the specific kind of scholarship embodied in *The Decision*, the physical setting depicted in *The Dandies* (plate 16) is just a "made-up" location, though it is based on the general characteristics of the south-central Montana region where Holm was raised and which is home to the Crow Nation. Holm conceived the image mainly as an opportunity to display a lot of 1870s-period finery and equipment, and he chose the role of the camp dandies to exhibit as many beautifully decorated pieces as could be imagined. The Plains style of sinew-backed, sheep-horn or elk-antler hunting bows has been the subject of several of Holm's experimental productions (he's made at least three working examples), and he naturally needed to have the appropriate sort of container in which to keep his most successful finished bow. The Crow/Plateau–style otter-skin bow-case quiver shown on the person of the mounted dandy in this picture is painted from the one that Holm made for his own bow, which was based on a number of original examples.[13] The Crow/Plateau–style bandoleer made by Mark Miller in trade for *Purifying the Shield* (plate 14) is worn over the shoulder of the dismounted Crow, who also is holding a Northwest Trade Gun in a fine Crow-style beaded gun case. This was painted after one made largely by Holm, with the addition of some beaded pieces made by his friend Louie Jull. The rawhide bull-elk love-medicine charm held by the mounted dandy was made by Mark Miller as a gift to the Holms (and has been employed by them as a Christmas tree ornament). The men's trade cloth and beaded leggings are based on original examples in the Holm collection, while the Osage orange-wood quirt, fancy hairpieces, and the skunk-skin ankle pendant were made by Holm after examples that have survived from the 1870s, the general period of the picture. Only three and one half pairs of such ankle pendants exist today in various collections, and he made the one depicted in this painting to match the surviving, incomplete half pair.

Holm selected late-afternoon or evening light for the scene, to best exhibit the naturally bright colors and shadows of this time of day, and he included several micro-views of camp life among the tipis in the valley. Among these are two women carrying firewood back to their lodges, medicine bundles tied to poles on the backs of two tipis, horses grazing nearby, and one man looking up into the setting sun to check out the two fancy-dressed strangers who are surveying the camp. Perhaps it is his daughter that one of the men has come a-courting. This is an intimate picture of what may have been a commonplace evening in a Crow summer camp, unfettered by the imaginable pressures of the outside world, and brimming over with what must have been the exquisite pleasures of just such a moment.

On the Northwest Coast of the eighteenth and early nineteenth centuries, the artists on several explorers' journeys produced drawings of First Peoples' war parties in the distinctive kind of canoe depicted in *Raven Warrior* (plate 17). None of them, however, seems to have composed his images from the imminent, dramatic viewpoint of this picture, the immediacy of which, at the time, would have represented a most terrifying sight. Holm's rendering of this scene was created for the 1991 Raven theme show at Seattle's Stonington Gallery. The archaic style of vessel pictured here dropped out of use about the middle nineteenth century, and it survives today only as a relatively small number of Native-made models and in the aforementioned kinds of drawings. Captain George Vancouver's aide, Lieutenant Whidbey, described an encounter in 1794 with Tlingit fighters in such a canoe. When fired upon from the English ship, the Tlingit swiftly turned the high, wide bow of their canoe in line with the gunfire and paddled backward with all their might. Only their hands and paddles were showing on either side of the protective canoe bow (Vancouver 1801, vol. 6:22–23; Emmons 1991: 349). Canadian artist Paul Kane field-sketched several of these canoes and recorded the measurements of one at Ft. Victoria in 1846. The lines and sculptural movements of these canoes are fascinating, and strangely unusual in comparison with other Northwest Coast canoe shapes. Their antiquity and subsequent development are intriguing to contemplate. The general form is obviously related to the Nuu-chah-nulth/Makah style of vessel shape, but with significantly altered lines about the bow, and with a much wider geographic distribution at one time. The eighteenth-century style of bluntly pointed canoe paddles is in evidence here as well, as it was in *Potlatch Guests* (plate 6).

Holm made many preliminary sketches of the gun-toting warrior in the lead canoe and created a painted-matboard miniature of a Muhnka canoe as a model for the vessels in the picture. The gun, of course, is painted from Holm's own Northwest Gun collection, of which two were once of the early flintlock type shown here, though they were long ago converted to percussion-type locks.[14] The raven helmet, the painted skin tunic, and the other warrior's helmet in the picture are original concepts based on the characteristics of existing historic Tlingit pieces, but the sheathed, raven-headed dagger on the lead fighter is painted from a particular weapon in the Peabody Museum at Harvard University. The thin curtain of fog that lends the scene some of its quiet, dreamlike quality was inspired by similar conditions encountered on trips around the San Juan Islands in Holm's big Haida-style canoe. A fog-shrouded, trading-canoe trip in the Great Lakes area, the subject of a nineteenth-century painting Holm admired by Frances Hopkins (who was married to the clerk of the Hudson's Bay Company's Sir George Simpson), also brought inspiration for this aspect of *Raven Warrior*.

One of the few Holm paintings to have been reproduced as a limited edition lithograph, *Raven Warrior* is one of the most consistently popular images in his catalog of work. It illustrates his special abilities in a most understated way, creating a spare and direct composition enhanced by the veil of fog that diminishes the background to mere shadows and dim highlights. Given the time scale suggested by the materials in the picture, this could well represent the Tlingit approach toward the first Russian outpost on Baranof Island in Southeast Alaska, which was named Fort St. Michael. Located near the present-day Sitka Marine Highway terminal, this fur-trading bastion was destroyed by the Sitka Tlingit people in 1802. True to the late-eighteenth-century style of northern-Northwest Coast design, the various formline images in the picture display all the characteristics of objects that date from this period. Holm's facility with Northwest Coast art and design is legendary, in part because he has made examples of so many different types of traditional artifacts in so many different media (from innumerable objects in wood or horn, to silver, copper, and steel). Holm's work is also highly respected because of his uncanny ability to represent skillfully and accurately a broad variety of coastal styles, from that of the Columbia River area to Southeast Alaska. His hand and eye are those of a stylistic chameleon, able to switch effortlessly between very different individual or time-based variants on the Northwest Coast traditions, as if he were many different artists and people. In this painting, the old archaic forms of the early historic-period Tlingit styles displayed on the canoes, paddles, painted armor, and carved helmets of the war party even include minor stylistic variances from one canoe or one object to the other, just as they would if they had been made by different artists of the day. Holm is able to capture the most subtle essences of these early styles, which survive today in the oldest ethnographic objects collected in the historic period, making his designs appear in every line and detail as if they were produced by individual artists of two hundred or more years ago. This same skill also shows up in the different historic nuances of the bead and quill work that Holm creates and represents in his paintings of the Plateau and Plains cultures.

A number of other Northwest Coast–style artists in this century, both Native and non-Native, have experimented with a range of First Nations styles and individual artist's traits of the past, expressing these various historic nuances and styles either as spontaneous creations or in the course of restoration and replication. In fact, these are skills pioneered in the 1950s by Mungo Martin and his assistants at the Royal British Columbia Museum and the UBC Museum of Anthropology (the first of whom were Doug Cranmer, Mungo's son David, Henry Hunt, and Tony Hunt). Perhaps no other artists today, however, have developed the level of ability that approaches the broad-ranging, masterful facility with these kinds of expression that is demonstrated on a day-to-day basis in the works of Bill Holm.

Another example of Holm's style-facility is illustrated in the leap of a hundred years and over five hundred miles to the time and setting of *Approach to Tsakhees*, 1890 (plate 18). Houses, canoe types, regalia, and the people themselves in this picture appropriately and elegantly reflect the characteristics of this period and location. The village is Fort Rupert, a site developed by the Hudson's Bay Company in 1849. The area was chosen due to its proximity to an open coal seam, which for many years provided a power source for the steam engine of the HMS *Beaver*, the first motorized trading vessel to work the Northwest Coast. The Kwaguł band of the Kwakwa̲ka'wakw Nation, formerly living at Kalokwis (Crooked Beach) on Turnour Island, moved to the foreshore adjacent to the HBC trading fort. Part of the stockade and a blockhouse from this establishment can be seen in the left background of this picture. The Kwaguł built their houses facing Beaver Harbour, above the beach with a creek running parallel along it, from which the village took its Kwakwala name, Tsakhees.

Today the original big-houses are gone, and the creek no longer parallels the beachfront, having been re-routed by a particularly large runoff one year that cut through straight to the tidewaters.[15] The residents of this recently expanded, major Kwakwa̱ka'wakw population and ceremonial center dedicated a new, very impressive big-house for ceremonial use in 1995. The interior houseposts and frontal decoration, the sculptural representation of a Sisiutl, were designed by Chief Tony Hunt, and were executed under his direction by a number of his relatives and associates. Many prominent Kwakwa̱ka'wakw artists live and work in Fort Rupert today. Like Tony Hunt, a number of these artists are direct descendants of Tlingit/Scottish ethnographer George Hunt.

Photographs of Tsakhees from the 1890s show clearly the many traditional houses and the tall, totemic-emblem poles that Holm has represented in this scene, although the vantage point of those pictures was from the beach itself and necessarily showed the village mostly from the side. Using those photographs as references, Holm shifted the view to coincide with the perspective of this painting. He painted the background first — the houses with the glow of firelight from within, the many people in detailed regalia anticipating the arrival of the guests, and the village canoes hauled up mostly stern first in the traditional fashion (to protect the fragile cutwaters, and so that they were ready for instant launch). Some of the canoes are covered with canvas to protect them from the drying and cracking effects of the sun. Having participated for over twenty years in the annual re-creation of just such a scene at the Henderson Camps/Camp Nor'wester, Holm knows with great familiarity the view from within such canoes.

Beginning in 1955, with the completion of the Holms' big-house at Henderson Camps/Camp Nor'wester on Lopez Island, Mungo Martin and his family were invited by the Holms and the Hendersons (and later by the Nor'wester staff as well), to put up a "play" potlatch at the camp. Kwakwa̱ka'wakw people came to sing and dance for memories' sake, without the underlying cultural business that was and is the backbone of the traditional potlatch. Special Kwakwala names were given by some elders to the Holm family and other participants on these occasions. Over most of the ensuing twenty-five summers, as many as forty-five Kwakwa̱ka'wakw elders and young people traveled for the weekend from Fort Rupert, Alert Bay, and Victoria to sing, dance, and laugh, and to paddle in the two Holm canoes. They reveled in the recollection and celebration of some of their most glorious and inspiring memories from a time known as *kwiskwa̱lyagwuła*, "the bygone days of the old people."

Privileged to have been there during ten or more of those events-out-of-time, with the old-timers "in charge" of the days and nights, I can still hear the voices and see the graceful, elegant steps of those who came to honor and celebrate with their friends and hosts for the occasions, Bill and Marty Holm (and the camp staff members). Their songs and laughter still reverberate from the sides of the little cove where the big-house sat.[16]

The list of honored guests at these events included Jonathan Hunt, Thomas and Emma Hunt, Bill Hunt, Tony Hunt, Adatsa (Peter) and Duda Smith, J. J. and Mrs. James Wallas, Dick Willy, Sandy Willy, Jim King, Aho Alfred, Ada Cook, Dzamaga (Dorothy Hawkins), Gwuntilakw (Agnes Cranmer), Katy Scow, and dozens more. Instead of the smiling, awe-struck faces of the camp kids gathered on the beach at Lopez, I imagine that, in their minds' eye, they saw the view painted in *Approach to Tsakhees* (or to Yalis, or to Ba'as, or to Gwayasdams villages). They used to say, "We do things here that haven't happened in fifty or sixty years!" And their laughter and the smiles on their faces would say even more. Now, happily, the new generations of Kwakwaka'wakw dancers, singers, and artists carry on where the members of this generation (those born in the nineteenth century) left off. Some of the present generation who are prominent in the current, vital expression of traditional Kwakwaka'wakw ceremonialism attended the Lopez play-potlatches as very young people accompanying the elders. These artists and ceremonial-ists today invite the Holms to many of their own contemporary potlatches, and they seat them as guests of honor among the chiefs and important singers.

Beginning with a sketch made while traveling as a resource person on a Northwest Coast cruise ship, and refining the idea with a watercolor study, Holm coalesced the im-ages and experiences of those special years into the composition of *Approach to Tsakhees*. In this painting, Holm has created one of the most intimate and involved viewpoints in all of his work: as the viewer, you are sitting right in one of the canoes, gently rocked by the rhythm of the song as it is tapped out by the paddlers and sent resonating through the hull of your craft. The details are meticulous: SuperKen modeled the peace dance head-dress, its frontlet painted from one that Holm made in 1967, based on old-time examples. The button robe and dancing apron are based on Holm's own, made over the years for use at the Lopez potlatches. The dress and the faces of the canoeists are drawn from old photos and from the visages of those whom Holm has known in the course of his decades-long relationship with the Kwakwaka'wakw people.

On the opposite side of the visitor-host equation, and back again five or six hundred miles to the north, *The Inviter* (plate 19) stands in welcome on the beach, waiting to receive his waterborne guests. The scene here, though, is set at some imaginary village in the Southeast Alaska archipelago. This is a land where spruce and hemlock forests crowd the few shallow beaches on a mostly steep and rocky shore, and where the endur-ing snowline hovers all winter long around the 2,000-foot level, often just a few hundred yards behind the tideline. This could be the 1860s in Wrangell, or Kake, or Tongass, when the Tlingit were still the undisputed masters of their northern world. Or it could be only yesterday in Haines, or Sitka, or Angoon, among people who have held onto their heirlooms and who still practice the privileges of their ancestors, in a territory that still displays a great deal of its spectacular natural glory.

The Chilkat robe in the picture is painted from one that has been in the Holm collection for over thirty years, a particularly finely woven piece of work featuring some of the most smoothly shaped lines, curves, and design forms of any such robes extant. Holm's trademark zeal for precision is apparent here. Not only is the weaver's fine rendering of the design itself perfectly represented in this painting, but the subtle details of relief that the weaving techniques create on the surface of the robe have been depicted, as have the faint shadows that delineate the raised texture of the vertical braids on each design form. Chilkat weaving is still another traditional technology with which Holm is experienced. In the 1960s, he visited with an elder Tlingit woman in Haines, Alaska, by the name of Jennie Thlunaut (then Jennie Marks). Jennie Thlunaut had woven many Chilkat robes and tunics in her lifetime of experience with these complex techniques, and she was at the time the last surviving traditional carrier of this knowledge. The words she shared with Holm, and his careful notes, inspired him to create a small sample-weaving—enough to provide an insider's understanding of the process. Years later, he shared those experiences and notes with several people who went on to weave a number of complete projects and to teach, in their turn, many new weavers in the techniques. Among such weavers are Cheryl Samuel, Dorica Jackson, and Jeannie Stewart. Jennie Thlunaut, who passed away in 1986, herself conducted several apprenticeships, and a workshop in Haines in 1985 passed her valuable knowledge on among newly interested Tlingit and Haida weavers. Today a slowly expanding group of devotees maintains and furthers this respected and honored tradition, creating new pieces for traditional use as well as for sale to collectors.

Holm posed for photographs with the robe, hat, and rattle at Goose Point on Lopez Island, where he painted *The Inviter.* For the background, however, he supplanted the Lopez Island scene with appropriate Southeast Alaskan environmental characteristics. The hat, based on the general appearance of a number of old clan heirlooms from various locations, was made for the sitting with a painted matboard cone and a cut-out and shaded matboard dorsal fin. Each was painted to imitate the styles of the fully decorated Tlingit hats made of wood or spruce root that are known from the mid-nineteenth century.[17] The formline image on the hat in this painting replicates beautifully the old, classic Tlingit styles that were prevalent in the early nineteenth century, a precious few examples of which remain in Tlingit use and custodianship in the region. The precise representation of the odd, foreshortened view of the raven rattle in the inviter's hand was facilitated with the help of one that Holm had made in the 1960s, and the inviter's long, beaded shirt was based on an old example from his collection. The striking appearance of the great white shark-tooth earring was modeled after an old pair that Holm purchased from a Tlingit student of his at the University of Washington.

The masterful and inspiring work of the Kwakwaka'wakw artist known as Hiḥlamas, or Willie Seaweed (1873–1967), has been one of the strongest and most intensely personal interests of Holm's professional career. The mounting of the important 1983 exhibition and Holm's accompanying book, *Smoky-Top: The Art and Times of Willie Seaweed*, marked the culmination of his nearly thirty years of study of the remarkable work of this quiet, highly traditional artist and 'Nak'waxda'x̱w chief.

Holm had an opportunity to meet the elderly carver and ceremonialist at Seaweed's Blunden Harbour home in 1959. That year, Holm traveled by seine boat to the remote village on the British Columbia mainland. He was included by the chiefs on an inviting trip for a potlatch to be given on Turnour Island by a group of cultural leaders anchored by Mungo Martin. Seaweed welcomed the party of inviters into his home, where he sang and danced in honor of their visit. In 1966, and again in 1968, Holm was extremely fortunate to acquire a *hamsamhl* (a mask of the hamat'sa series) that had been carved by this greatly admired and respected artist. These are the two masks depicted in *Hamsamala* (plate 20), displayed there in the way that they were originally intended to be seen. The masks are manipulated in graceful motions by skilled dancers who put on a magical performance, replicating the quirky, birdlike movements that are associated with these cedar bark–clad, monster-bird images.

These two masks arrived in Holm's possession from separate and very circuitous routes, and yet they appear to have been made by Seaweed during the same time-period of his career, if not originally as parts of the same set. Though not as flamboyantly elaborate as certain other later masks by Seaweed (Holm 1983: cat. 67, 68), these examples represent two of the most elegantly conceived and refined versions of the many Hamsamala masks that Seaweed produced in his long working life. Living daily in the company of these fantastic images not only influenced Holm's appreciation for and understanding of the beauty and uniqueness of Seaweed's innovative and superbly executed art, but it inspired him as well to carve the third member of the traditional trio of cannibal-bird images, the raven mask of Baxbakwalanuksiwe' (figure 18). Using the two original Seaweed masks as stylistic guides, Holm carved and painted the raven mask to complement as closely as possible the original two. Seaweed's refined technique shows through in Holm's work, and the stylistic integrity of this raven mask within the trio is a remarkable tribute by Holm to Seaweed, the Master.

In *Hamsamala* (plate 20), Holm has combined his admiration for Seaweed's work with his own firsthand experience of and familiarity with the traditional events and per-

18 / *Raven* hams̲a̲ml *mask, 1983, carved by Holm in the 1940s-period style of Willie Seaweed, Naxwakdaxw artist from Blunden Harbour, British Columbia. This mask accompanies two masks made by Seaweed in the Holm collection, completing the trio of Hamat'sa-associated cannibal birds that often make a traditional set. Holm purchased a Willie Seaweed Crooked-beak mask in 1966 from George Terasaki, and he received a Huxwhukw mask by the same artist from Anne Gerber, in recognition of his years of assistance with her husband Sidney's Northwest Coast art collection. Holm made the raven mask as a study of Seaweed's carving style, and also to be able to perform with it at the opening of the Pacific Science Center/Burke Museum exhibit of Seaweed's work, "Smoky-Top: The Art and Times of Willie Seaweed," curated by Holm.*

19 / *Aleut-style bentwood hunting hat, 1982. Hemlock, ivory, paint, nylon "sea lion" whiskers, beads. Holm made this hat as an experiment in the sophisticated traditional style of their manufacture. The wood must be carved extremely thin in particular places to replicate the sculptural characteristics of the original hats. This hat appears in* The Sea Otter Dart *(plate 21).*

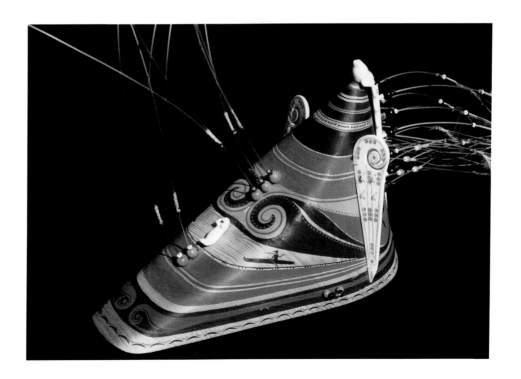

formances of a Kwakwaka'wakw potlatch. This composition honors the visionary images of the two Seaweed masks in Holm's collection, and also the personalities of two of his most admired and appreciated teachers, Willie Seaweed and Mungo Martin. The latter, in addition to being a highly respected artist and ceremonial treasure-keeper, was Holm's introduction into the unique and enlightening world of the Kwakwaka'wakw culture. In the picture, Seaweed stands on the right of the group of singers, wearing a cedar bark head ring and neck ring, with his song leader's baton raised as he calls out the words to the following verse of the dance accompaniment. Martin is seated among the singers, on the right of Willie Seaweed, keeping the time of the song and watching the enjoyment on the faces of his companions. The recollections of many of Holm's old friends and acquaintances are embodied in the full assembly of personages represented in this dramatic image.

As viewers, we are drawn into the picture by the nearness of the Hamsamala dancer in the foreground. We might actually be in the scene, like one of the attendants—those who accompany the performers about the house and assist by guiding them on their transit of the floor, and who back them up during the sitting portion of the traditional choreography. (This function is demonstrated by the blue-shirted attendant crouched behind the Huxwhukw dancer on the lower right of the picture). SuperKen posed wearing the Crooked Beak mask for the image of the near figure, shown poised on one knee as some dancers are in this portion of the performance. The position of the seated dancer in the Huxwhukw mask was painted after a photograph that Holm had made of a dancer at a potlatch in the village of He'gams in 1986. Tufts of eagle down placed on the heads of the dancers have drifted to the floor, representing a sacred symbol of peace and healing in the Winter Ceremonial.

Illuminated by the firelight, the dramatic carvings here dominate the scene. The three powerful spirals of the Crooked Beak mask in the foreground are highlighted by the backlight of the fire's bright glow. Each circular form is perfectly balanced by the others: the backward curl of the "ears" above the eyebrows; the downward spiral of the beak on the small face on the mask's lower jaw; and the full, round, massive spiral of the nostril complex on the mask arching out and down to touch the forward edge of the broad, short beak of the cannibal-bird image. The eccentric circles of the figure's eye anchor the design movements of the total image.

On the houseposts in the background, the figure of the Qolus, or thunderbird, holds the massive weight of the entire house structure on its head. Its huge wings sweep out to each side as if to maintain its balance on the head of the grizzly bear below, seen sitting on its haunches with forepaws raised in a revealing gesture.

For the house interior, Holm has re-created certain features of Chief John Scow's

46

Raven House of Gwayasdams village, Gilford Island, British Columbia, though the scale of the carved post and the size of the house in the painting are slightly larger than the original features of the Raven House. The architectural structure of the house is clearly visible in the blazing firelight, including the texture of the adzed patterns on the surface of the main support beams, skillfully applied in alternating directions. The Qolus and Grizzly Bear houseposts, from which the tall, bold carving in the picture has been painted, were carved in 1907 by Hemasilakw, or Arthur Shaughnessy (Brown, ed., 1995: 242–51). The strong, dramatic features of this carving have been further accentuated by the elaborate painting that Hemasilakw applied to the sculptured forms. The white-painted background of the designs punches up the contrast of the painted imagery and represents a largely twentieth-century artistic technique that is also reflected in the painting of the two 1940s-vintage Willie Seaweed masks in the picture. The cloth curtain on the right of the painting, depicting a raven and a Sisiutl, is reproduced from one that was photographed in use in the Raven House in 1946, and which is now in the Denver Museum of Natural History. The wing of another bird image painted on cloth shows from behind the foreground dancer. This one is also based on a particular old screen, and is indicative of the early twentieth-century Kwakwaka'wakw style. The original Raven House was dedicated in 1916 and remained intact through the 1940s. Prior to 1954, the house walls and roof were dismantled, though the framework of the building remained standing on Gilford Island until 1966, when it was sold to John H. Hauberg of Seattle by William Scow, son of the original owner. From 1972–1991, a reconstruction of this house, combined with the frontal image of its predecessor, the Sea Monster House, stood in the Life Sciences Building of the Pacific Science Center in Seattle. Reconstructed by a joint effort of the Pacific Science Center and the Burke Museum, the interior of the Raven House also served as the exhibition venue for the presentation of the *Smoky-Top* retrospective. Through Hauberg's generosity, the four original carved posts of the Raven House are now in the Seattle Art Museum's third-floor Native American exhibit area.

Ingenious traditional wood technologies are the fascination of many, though the experience that Bill Holm has developed with so many different techniques from so many culture areas is certainly rare and outstanding in this field. The fabulously embellished and ingeniously constructed bentwood hunting hats that were the exclusive development of Aleutian craftsmen have long intrigued Holm. He had seen many of these now very rare and fragile headgear in the museums and institutional storage areas of Europe while on his research sabbatical in 1976, and on consultation trips for the *Crossroads of Continents* exhibition in 1988. In that (or the following) year, Holm thinly shaved down a split board

47

of hemlock into the intricately formed shape of one of these hats. He then steamed the wood and gently bent it into the complex curves and valleys of this light and delicate headgear. The hunting hat depicted in *The Sea Otter Dart* (plate 21) was the result, with its fine painting, carved and engraved ivory volutes, trade beads, and sea lion whiskers attached in the elaborate fashion of this unique tradition (figure 19). Holm elongated the proportions of his own hat for the picture, to be more in keeping with the scale of original examples of these hats.

Preparing to paint this picture some three years later, Holm also carved and constructed the traditional form of hunting dart and atlatl, or throwing board, depicted in this view of an eighteenth-century hunting party. The paddle was modeled after one from the Aleutian area housed in the Burke Museum, and the spray skirt that keeps the paddler dry in his baidarka seat was made up from those visible in old photographs. In order to replicate the appearance of the hunter's parka, originally made from strips of seal intestine that were processed, dried, and sewn together into a waterproof garment, Holm marked up the look of the seam lines in chalk on a buff-colored nylon jacket. The delicate hold of the hunter's hand on the atlatl and dart was a little too complex even for the multi-talented SuperKen, so Holm modeled the weapon system himself for photographs that clearly detailed the aspects he needed to represent in the painting.

Again, as the viewers of this scene, we are brought in close, able to see the exquisite detail of the hunter, his equipment, and the spectacular headgear. In the distance we see his companions, in a single and a double-seat baidarka, and we also get a strong visual and emotional sense of the isolated, unforgiving, and yet bounteous sea environment in which these peoples made their homes.

Bill Holm's fascination with Northwest Coast dugout canoes and the inventive processes required in their making were the clear inspiration for *Spreading the Canoe* (plate 22). Canoe makers from all parts of the coast explored the forests for that one-in-a-hundred, old-growth ancestor-tree from which to carve their next traditional watercraft. Not just any big tree would do, even today. Trees that had developed a large girth with a solid center (or at least without extensive rot in the middle), without broken tops to let in water and fungus spores, and growing in quiet, sheltered locations protected from storm winds — these were the trees for which the canoe makers searched. It was (and is) often in very limited zones where such conditions are more frequently or consistently encountered. Usually found some distance from the canoe makers' home village, the tree would be felled, shaped, and rough-hollowed right where it had been felled. When it was down to perhaps six inches or less in thickness overall, it would be pulled, pushed, and skidded over smaller downed trees and along open creekbeds to the edge of the saltwater. From

20 / The Holm studio, north of Seattle. Built between 1969 and 1974, this 25 × 30-foot building is based on the six-beam Haida-style house architecture of the northern Northwest coast. Windows along the southwest wall provide natural light when needed. The studio was constructed over many weekends, with all the work being done by Holm, frequently assisted by Steve Brown. In order to raise the corner posts, gable plates, and rafter beams, Holm designed an ingeniously guyed gin-pole with a hand-crank winch. With this simple lift, Holm and Brown raised and placed all the posts and beams for the framework. The gin pole itself then became the ridge beam of the house. The exterior pole was raised into place in 1984. Holm carved the 35-foot pole from the back side of a cedar log, which also provided material for the Tsimshian-style pole he carved for the Burke Museum in 1971.

21 / Detail of beaver image on the studio frontal pole. Emblems on the pole are based on those of an argillite model totem carved by the nineteenth-century Haida artist Charles Edenshaw. Holm acquired the argillite model in 1982 and decided to replicate its imagery on the full-size pole. The style in which he carved the studio-pole figures, however, is his own take on the Haida monumental totem tradition, and is very different from the Edenshaw style of argillite pole carving.

there, it would be towed by another canoe back to the village beach for final refinement, steam-spreading, and complete fitting-out.

Canoe steaming is an hours-long, somewhat tedious process that can literally make or break the final canoe. Patience and experience pay off well, though, and the excitement of seeing the hull change so beautifully and drastically in shape is a reward like few others. In this picture, Holm has re-created such an event as witnessed hundreds of times over in the nineteenth century (as well as earlier), when canoes were made and traded by master builders over hundreds of miles of coastal territory. The front of his Haida-style studio (built between 1969 and 1974) served as the model for the village houses, although he beefed up the relative size of the structural beams for the picture. At the center of the house, the frontal totem pole has the same carved images as the one that Holm completed and raised at his studio in 1984. The painted version, however, was done with the addition of black, red, and blue painted colors and the oval entry opening, which the actual pole does not have. The studio pole is thirty-five-feet tall and was carved from the back half of the log from which Holm had replicated a Tsimshian-style pole for the Burke Museum collection some ten years before. The other two totemic sculptures in this picture are imaginary in form, based on carvings from the general nineteenth-century Haida tradition.

Holm has said that his challenge to himself in this canvas was "to present the billowing steam, the smoke and the fires, the colors and textures of the various woods, the characteristics of the houses and the beach, and something of the whole experience of the process itself for the viewer." He says that he could not resist including the observer off to the side, and nearly painted in two more old-timers sitting next to the house, watching over the young men who are involved in their work down the beach. His deep admiration for the ingenuity of the canoe makers, and for the visual and architectural mastery of the house builders, is clearly in evidence here, in a picture that celebrates the inventive brilliance and finely hewn workmanship of the Northwest Coast cultures.

So many of Bill Holm's paintings, in spite of their apparent focus on the decorated objects and physical trappings of the individual cultures involved, are really about people, individual people, those who made up the households, bands, villages, and language families of the North American First Nations. In the small vignette entitled *A Chief by Means of Deeds* (plate 23), it is in fact the person behind the story who is the real subject of the picture. The finery he possesses, which he displays with such strength and dignity, is only part of the story: it is simply a further manifestation and a visual expression of the status, respect, and admiration that his actions and deeds have earned among his people.

22 / *The rear inner wall of the Holm studio, with painted and relief-carved designs on the cedar house screen and a twelve-foot housepost at the center. Holm was assisted by Steve Brown in painting and carving the interior screen (1974), while his wife Marty helped to finish the carving of the housepost (1978).*

23 / *Bill Holm in his studio, with SuperKen sitting for* The High Ridge *(plate 42). Painted parfleches, warbonnet cases, Mark Miller's transmontane-style bandoleer bag, and Holm's quill-wrapped horsehair shirt hang on the studio wall. (Photo by Marcia Iverson)*

The beaded and ermine-tube decorated shirt and the beaded leggings in this picture are drawn from old examples of the types. The man's moccasins are based on a pair from the Crow tradition, now housed at the Carnegie Museum, Pittsburgh. The shield is representative of the kinds of general imagery that are typical of the region and period. The specific design on this shield was revealed to Holm while he was on an airplane trip across this area of the country. On this particular nighttime flight, he saw the northern lights aglow in the sky and also the eerie beacons of the lighted towns on the ground below. His impressions of this remarkable scene were later transformed into the shield painting.

Each eagle feather in this picture — on the lance, the shield, the horse's forelock, and the chief's hair — is, as always, painted from an individual feather in Holm's collection. The unique style of hair ornament, made with beads, dentalia shells, and feathers, was painted using one of several such ornaments that Holm has made in the traditional Crow fashion. The Crow/Hidatsa–style, red paint–daubed hairpiece or trailer is based on old museum examples and on photographs of the style from the nineteenth century. Such a trailer also appears in plate 14, on the man who is "smudging" the Crow warrior's shield. The tied-up tail and red-painted dashing on the horse are based on old traditions, and the horse itself is modeled on photos taken in 1943 of Holm's cousin's beloved steed, "Snaggy." In addition, Holm has lived in one of his tipis for nearly every summer since 1946, so the pitch, the taut form, and the way the light plays on these wonderful, portable dwellings (like those shown here and in others of his paintings) are fondly familiar to his eye.

Always reserved about his own skills as a painter, Holm is forever quick to praise those in the field whose work he admires most. Among those painters in various styles from whom he derives a large measure of inspiration are Ned Jacob, Mark Myers, and especially Howard Terpning. Although Holm works almost exclusively in acrylic paints, because he appreciates the quick-drying layerability of this medium, which suits his approach to his work, he decided to attend an oil painting workshop hosted by Terpning in Kerrville, Texas, in 1993. Two oil paintings from this workshop experience are *Waiting out the Storm* (plate 24) and *The Taunt* (plate 25).

For *Waiting out the Storm*, Bill dressed SuperKen in a Hudson's Bay blanket pinned over his shoulder in the fashion typical of the middle nineteenth century. Using an original old Nuu-chah-nulth/Makah paddle from his own collection, and the image of an early type of black-rimmed spruce root hat typical of this area, Holm equipped his traveling canoe captain as were many in that day. He employed the skills learned in Terpning's workshop to render the dark, wild sky and turbulent waters in a manner which he feels is a significant departure from his earliest paintings. In this piece, we see the major geographical points of the west coast of Vancouver Island diminishing in the distance, and a look of experience, wisdom, and dignified bravery on the determined visage of the energetic captain. The graceful, expressive lines that make up the abstract creature-form of the traditional Nuu-chah-nulth-style canoe bow behind him appear to yearn out to sea with equal energy and determination.

Pivotal, defining historic moments hold a deep fascination for Holm. *The Decision* (plate 15) portrays one such turning point. *The Taunt* (plate 25) also captures the haunting momentum of that instant when an otherwise common and undistinguished military sortie was transformed into a historic tragedy. In this case, Captain William Fetterman's pride and headstrong determination created a major command blunder that has been branded as infamous ever since. As he had with *The Decision*, Holm first rendered the incident in this picture in a drawing made while he was in junior high school, circa 1938. In his 1993 homage to the scene, he sets the viewpoint from among the group of mounted and seemingly reckless warrior-decoys, those who teased and tempted the captain and his column of soldiers into crossing their point of no return: the crest of Lodge Trail Ridge. At this moment, the fate of the small military force was sealed. Their commander's doomed engagement would be memorialized in history as "The Fetterman Massacre."

Historical photographs and those made on his own visits to the Bozeman Road site of this incident in Wyoming set the look of the background for this picture. The twin wagon ruts that identify the "road" can be seen between the members of the decoy party. On one of Holm's winter visits to the area, a light snow had fallen, just like the one documented in the picture. Clouds of moist vapor are exhaled by horses and warriors on that cold December solstice day. The bold and intimidating movements of the warriors are acted out in tantalizing nearness to the futile puffs of gunsmoke that issue from the soldier's weapons on the ridge. You can sense and feel the pregnancy of the event and can almost hear the calls and taunts of the decoys and the snorting breaths and prancing hooves of their horses. Back at Fort Phil Kearney, Colonel Carrington's jaw must have dropped in horrified disbelief and anger when he learned of the fate of his men.

As usual, SuperKen posed with various outfits for pictures of each of the four taunters. The yellow ochre–colored shirt on the far left is based on one Holm had made many years earlier, modified in its design to replicate more accurately the 1866 Cheyenne style. The shield design is from the artist's imagination, and the leggings and other articles worn by the warriors are adapted from pieces in his collection.

A less overtly violent, but equally precipitous moment is immortalized in *Nez Perce Scouts at the Musselshell River* (plate 26). Aware of the historical background outlined in Holm's caption for the picture, we know that this is the calm before the final, tragic, decisive storm. The familiar environment of south-central Montana is the setting in which this stage of the Nez Perce journey was realized, and Holm's many experiences along the Musselshell River have given him vivid mind-pictures from which to paint its autumn features. The hopeful alertness and fatigued relief visible on the warriors' faces are tellingly indicative of their plight. For the viewer, foreknowledge evokes heightened sympathy with the moment.

Subtle references to their battle equipment are recorded in a natural and casual manner: the characteristic shape of its brass butt plate identifies the Winchester 1866 rifle, slung in a case over the shoulders of the forward trail scout, and his cartridge belt, loaded with the short, fat cases of .44-Henry rimfire ammunition used in his rifle, binds an extra blanket about his waist. The short barrel and fore-end stock of the 1873 Springfield carbine are visible as it lies casually across the thighs of the second scout, and his traditional bowcase-quiver is ready over his shoulders. Had their war chief Looking Glass remained as wary as the lead scout here appears to be, he might not have succumbed to a false sense of security when their last engagement with the U.S. Army yielded no apparent pursuit. Had it been so, the large band of battle-weary survivors might have maintained their established pace toward freedom, outdistanced Colonel Miles, and achieved their safety in Canada. Chief Joseph might never have had to deliver his "fight no more forever" speech.

Not surprisingly, enthusiasts and collectors of Plains and Plateau First Peoples art are some of Holm's most enthusiastic patrons. For particular members of this audience, he created a series of images that primarily highlighted the beauty and details of the traditional objects depicted in each portraitlike canvas. Many of the decorated objects in these pictures are painted from original examples. Some of these objects are owned by the patrons and some come from the Holm's collection. Other pieces are drawn from ones that Holm has previously made. *The Mountain Lion Skin Quiver* (plate 27) is one of the latter, based on a few surviving examples of these utilitarian artworks. His description of the type in the picture caption clearly reveals his admiration and attraction to the tradition. SuperKen modeled a moosehide robe in place of the painted buffalo example of the finished painting, and Holm invented the scenes of the warrior's exploits immortalized on its brain-tanned surface. The moccasins in this picture are the quill-wrapped horsehair ones that Holm had made a couple of years earlier. *The Mountain Lion Skin Quiver* was originally done "on speculation" as a fun picture just to highlight the style of spectacular bowcase-quiver that is the focus of the image, and which Holm had recently completed. This canvas was sold, through the Sun Valley gallery of Paul Raczka, to the collectors Wayne and Nancy Badovinus. Charmed by the painting, the Badovinuses went on to commission two additional canvases: *Blue Beaded Guncase* and *Brass Finery*. For *Blue Beaded Guncase* (plate 28), Holm included several pieces of his own making: the straightup bonnet, the loop necklace, the medicine-bundle parfleches, and the breechclout. The shirt is painted from an original one that a friend had purchased in 1942, had kept for fifty years, and had then presented to Holm in appreciation for a personal favor. The guncase itself is based on an old Blackfeet example in the Holms's collection. *Brass Finery* (plate 29) highlights a number of examples of highly valued brass work, its decoration punctuated by furniture tacks of brass. In this picture, the split-horn bonnet, the 1866 Winchester, and the tack-studded quirt all represent articles from the collection of the owners of the painting. At some past point in time, the brass and bead–decorated belt drop on the warrior had been fastened to the wooden quirt, so Holm took the opportunity presented by the painting to return it (at least figuratively) to its more usual place as a traditional Crow-style belt drop.

The very unusual headdress represented in *Bear Straightup Bonnet* (plate 30) is painted after a recently made artifact owned by Paul Raczka, who commissioned this painting, and the chief's leggings are drawn from an original northern Plains pair in the Holm collection. The moccasins, shirt, and shield have been invented, based of course on the prevailing styles of the day, and each feather is once again painted from the real thing. Fortunately for him and his viewers, Holm really likes to paint feathers!

Lushootseed Research is an organization dedicated to the preservation of the Puget Sound Salish language and the traditional stories that have been its vehicle for thousands of years. The person who anchors this diverse and very productive group of individuals is Vi Hilbert, a talented and respected elder of the Upper Skagit Tribe.[18] Many of the volunteers and contributors to Lushootseed Research are Hilbert's present or former students. Holm painted *Family Outing* (plate 31) for a 1993 fundraising auction to benefit Lushootseed Research, and he elected to represent a scene that would have repeated itself time and again in the Puget Sound region: a Puget Salish family traveling by canoe in one of the innumerable waterborne passages of their livelihoods. Holm's caption for the picture notes the time of year, and also the rolled-up cattail mats and baskets of provisions in the canoe. Perhaps the paddlers are carrying these as items of trade or gifting to friends or relatives in another village site, or they may be returning home from a spring fishing or hunting camp. The cattail mats provided coverings for a temporary shelter, and the baskets carried the dried preserves of their successful hunting or fishing.[19] A cedar bark woven hat covers the woman's head from the sun, and a tunic of the same material shrouds her shoulders. The men wear trade blankets about their waists as the warmth of the sun retreats, and they count on the energy expended in paddling to heat them internally as dusk approaches. A bright moon could illuminate their route over a great distance into the night, and an assisting tide might help to carry them farther than paddling alone would accomplish. Paul Kane, the nineteenth-century Canadian artist, noted a canoe trip in his journal of 1846 that left one morning from the HBC farm near the Nisqually River delta and traveled all night through Puget Sound, to arrive at Fort Victoria in the middle of the next afternoon, a distance of roughly one hundred nautical miles covered in about thirty-three hours.[20]

Though Holm's own Coast Salish–style canoe is 25 percent shorter than this approximately twenty-five-foot vessel, the experience of paddling it through these same waters no doubt influenced his selection of the scene's imagery and its sense of tranquility. In the distance, the glow of Mount Baker towers over the silhouettes of Burroughs, Allan, and Fidalgo islands, and the smooth sheen of the calm water brightly reflects the colors of the evening sky. The artist has remarked on the Luminist style of this small painting, and how the image was interpreted from the remembrance of many similar evenings on Goose Point, southeast Lopez Island, where he and his family frequently retire for their most peaceful and treasured times.

A similar image, made for a similar purpose, is depicted in *Easy Morning* (plate 32), another small canvas painted to benefit a fundraising auction. This auction was put together by Nuu-chah-nulth artist Art Thompson and others to assemble monies for a Native Student Center, to be built on the campus of Camosun College in Victoria, British Columbia, where Thompson had been a student.

This tranquil image depicts the smaller type of vessel known as *s'nagqiɫ*. (The "n" transmutes to "d" between the Halkomelem [*s'nagqiɫ*] and Lushootseed [*s'dagwiɫ*] versions of this word. See the discussion of plate 10 on page 30.) A man with striking features, a member of the Cowichan or other Halkomelem-speaking First Nations, pauses after one last stroke of the paddle to survey some aspect of his world from the gently gliding, dynamic form of his traditional canoe. The shape of his head reflects the practice of re-forming the crania of infants in specially designed cradleboards, a widespread tradition in the southern Northwest Coast region prior to the mid-nineteenth century. His mustache and narrow beard are also typical of First Peoples in this area of the continent. He wears an indigenous Coast Salish–style blanket fastened with a wood or bone pin over his shoulder. Such robes were woven on a two-bar, roller loom from mountain goat and/or dog's wool, with a little bit of geometric design in narrow bands of a contrasting color. A bright piece of abalone shell worn on his ear glints in the morning light, and a foggy haze obscures the details of the shoreline in the background. The only sounds are the trickle of water that drips from the end of his paddle, and the faint lapping of the water-ripples that are cut by the bow of his small, sure craft.

The small vignette entitled *Oh Yes! I Love You, Honey Dear* (plate 33) currently hangs in the Holms's kitchen. It is a bright tribute to the joyous spirit of the love songs performed with couples' dances among the Plains and Plateau peoples (often included in modern pow-wows), as well as to the deep feelings and dedicated character of the enduring bond between Bill and Marty Holm in the nearly fifty years of their marriage.

The singing of these kinds of love songs, and the dances they accompany, are always punctuated with bursts of laughter and the calls of good-natured teasing between friends and couples. For the Owl Dance, a graceful, turning step performed as couples circle about the dance grounds, the women select their dance partners. Any man who declines to dance with the one who chooses him is required to endure some mild and usually embarrassing penitence before the pow-wow crowd.

As a participant in pow-wow dances at the towns of Yakima and Toppenish for many years, Holm acquired several old pieces for his dancing outfits through that period. He produced examples himself of the types of artworks he admired most. These Plateau-style objects were also used to enrich the cultural offerings of the Henderson Camps/Camp Nor'wester summer programs, where the older units of campers have always lived in tipis during their stay at camp. Over the years, through trade or sale of some of the old pieces, the Holm collection of dancing outfits has continued to evolve in minor ways.

Holm once owned the leggings of the singer on the left, and he made this man's belt and the belt pouch with its design of an Appaloosa horse. Marty Holm made the belt drop that goes with them. The floral-beaded breechclout is an old original Plateau piece, to which beadworker Louie Jull added the loops of beads that encircle the flowers and the four flower stems that meet at the center design (thereby completing a more typical design-style). Holm made the loop necklaces, while the leggings of the singer on the right and the hairpipe bandoleer are old examples he purchased in eastern Washington many years ago. The belt and pouch of this singer are also original pieces of Plateau fine-work. (Some Nez Perce and other Plateau Nation men of today continue to dress for pow-wows in outfits with these kinds of features and component pieces, in addition to the more elaborate and specialized war-dance outfits of the men's traditional or fancy-dance categories). The coyote skin, otter-skin wraps, feathers, and plaid cloth breechclout are all painted from their actual counterparts, a fact that Holm feels brings a spirit of sincerity and accuracy to his process, as well as to the finished work.

Many of Holm's paintings have been motivated by an arrangement for a trade and in more than one instance he has produced a canvas in exchange for a good, old example of a Northwest Trade Gun. Jim Richardson, a friend of Holm's, owned an 1818-vintage musket, and he commissioned a painting on the general subject of "ships on the Northwest Coast" in trade for it. The result was Mexicana *and* Sutil *in Guemes Channel, June 11, 1792* (plate 34), a picture which, in addition to fulfilling the basic request, contains more than one interesting historic connection to the artist. Holm says he "heavily researched" the consummation of events that compose this particular image, beginning his studies a number of years before the idea of the painting itself was spawned. Accounts of this voyage mention the Spanish captains putting ashore near Watmough Head on southeast Lopez Island, where they set up for and made celestial observations to determine their longitude by watching the transit of the moons of Jupiter about their parent planet.[21]

Holm realized that the Spanish observations of 1792 had almost certainly been made from the low, open protrusion of land now known as Goose Point, part of the parcel of land that he and Marty had purchased as a cabin site in the 1960s. In 1992, out of respect for this bit of history, the Holms and some of their friends undertook a small celebration of the bicentennial of the Spanish landing. The Spanish flag in this picture was, in fact, given as a gift to Holm in honor of the occasion by his friend and colleague Jack Henry. With such an awareness of this particular event, there was little question which "ships on the Northwest Coast" would be portrayed in the painting commissioned in exchange for the Northwest Gun!

His interest spurred by the prospect of this trade, Holm studied the drawings of expedition artist José Cardero, who had illustrated the two ships and their passage through Guemes Channel, and the journal accounts from the ships' logs for details to include in the scene. Holm himself knew this location very well, having been by the same area perhaps hundreds of times. Anyone who has been aboard one of the Washington State Ferries bound from the San Juan Islands to Anacortes has also passed this spot, which is marked "Shannon Point" on navigational charts, just west of the ferry terminal.

Holm's research also put him in touch with Mark Myers, an accomplished artist of nautical history who had done the numerous detailed illustrations for John Harland's book *Seamanship in the Age of Sail* (Annapolis: Naval Institute Press, 1984). Holm and Myers had in fact been corresponding over time on a number of topics of interest to both men.

Holm had exchanged a great deal of information with Myers on the detailing of the archaic head-canoes and the Northwest Coast design style, which culminated in Myers's watercolor, entitled *Ononnistoy*, of Vancouver's ship *Discovery* at Port Stewart, Alaska.[22] Their correspondence included a fourteen-page letter from Myers on the details of the two ships. This postal conversation facilitated the re-painting of the structure of the mast on the *Mexicana* (the ship on the left). Cardero's drawing of the mast on this ship was done following its re-rigging during their stay at Nootka Sound, which was done in a technique that was very unusual in its day. Holm had initially painted the mast with the more common manner of fastening the top mast to the main mast at the maintop. Myers's letter assisted Holm in interpreting the Cardero drawing, and Bill repainted the mast based on these suggestions.

Another alteration, buried beneath the finished paint surface of this canvas, involves the approaching canoe. When I first saw this image in progress, the canoe was closer to the foreground, as are the subjects of many of Holm's paintings, entering the scene from the right of the picture. It evidently never looked 'quite right' to the artist in that orientation, and he moved the canoe with the four paddlers and elder leader to its present position. The finely woven hats and the robes of bear skin and wool show clearly in the midday light, and the beautiful sheer-curve of the canoe describes its seaworthy form. Beneath the reflection of the *Sutil*, visible on the glassy surface of the tide eddy that carried the vessel eastward, the first painted draft of the canoe and its occupants lies hidden.

Another of the pivotal historic moments that Holm has dramatized illustrates the first-ever sighting of a European ship by Vancouver Island First Peoples. To represent this unrecorded event, Holm chose to depict a Mowachaht (Nuu-chah-nulth) pelagic seal hunter, pausing in studied observation of the *First Sail* (plate 35), with no way of knowing that, from this day forward, the lives of the Mowachaht and the other Northwest Coast First Nations would be forever altered.[23] The image here portrayed eloquently communicates the depth and dramatic character of this pivotal and defining event, through the medium of a scene that is emotionally and visually understated.

Holm envisioned this complete scene while walking along Richmond Beach on a blustery day with the same kind of dark, roiling clouds seen here. He roughed-out the image in about fifteen minutes upon his return to the studio. The viewpoint of the picture is again up-close and is intuitively involved with the primary subject—the seal hunter and his canoe. We are passengers in his craft, part of his world, looking in the distance at a small and seemingly insignificant object as it approaches within the realm of the hunter. Dark, ominous skies, punctuated by bright highlights on the edge of the clouds, form a backdrop to the drama unfolding on the surface of the sea. The true import of this emissary from the outside world is nothing less than cataclysmic — as we know in retrospect. The hunter pauses in his time-honored pursuit, armed with the finely hewn technologies of his day: the elegant canoe and its sweet, springy, yew-wood paddle, the ingenious components of his harpoon, his beautiful cloak of yellowcedar bark, and the carved club carried to dispatch his quarry. The hunter's entire indigenous world is symbolized by the trappings of his life — seen here in a striking contrast to what we know lies behind the innocuous appearance of the distant vessel.

The powerful, diminishing lines of the canoe's gunwales are accentuated by the natural, delicate list of the hull. Perhaps the hunter has captured a seal that is already stored amidships, or the canoe is responding to the hunter's weight borne by his right foot. Though not dangerously tender, these vessels have an innate axial roll that does not affect their total seaworthiness but is naturally expressed when their load is even slightly off-centered. (This same effect can be seen in the lead vessel of *Raven Warrior* [plate 17] and its presence here comes about directly from Holm's experiences paddling the canoes of his own making.) The low lighting reveals bright colors, and the traditional details of the canoe's finish can be seen in the light and shadow of its interior. Straight, narrow rows of adze-marks cross the width of the hull from side to side, and fine knife-grooves parallel the upper rim, inside and below the gunwale's edge where the "paddle-piece" strips have been added (known as *tL'eixats* in the Makah language [Waterman 1920:16]). The carved groove in which the harpoon is rested while in transit can be seen between the textured tips of the gunwales on the rear surface of the bow flares.

These Spanish seamen, whose story is described in the picture's caption, in turn astounded the Nuu-chah-nulth with their ways. The name given to their kind in the Nuu-chah-nulth language became the identity by which Euro-Americans are still known today — *Mamahlni*, "those whose houses move about on the water." They seemed to have no home — no land that the Nuu-chah-nulth knew of, anyway — only the big ships that they lived on, from which they journeyed ashore only in short trips, for water or food or materials. What they brought with them would eventually transform everything in the seal hunter's world, to the point that only fragments survive today of what is represented in this image.

*Yakama Sunset* (plate 36) was painted for Natalie Linn, a well-known and knowledgeable collector/dealer from Portland, Oregon. Holm took the opportunity to focus on the style of Indian hemp and corn husk weavings unique to the Columbia Plateau, generally known as corn-husk bags. Originally made for the gathering and storage of indigenous roots, such as the bitterroot, cous, and camas, these bags had later become highly valued items of Plateau finery, to be worn and displayed at important festival occasions such as the pow-wows held annually in many inland First Peoples' communities along the Columbia drainage. The warm evening light and cool shadows bring out the varied colors in the woman's outfit and the designs on the many woven pieces.

The woman's hat is painted from one that was displayed in the ATOG exhibit at the Burke Museum in 1989 (Wright, ed., 1991:89, fig. 42). A very similar hat in the ATOG exhibit was collected along the Columbia River in 1792 by a member of Vancouver's expedition (ibid.: fig. 41). The woman's spectacular dress is more loosely based on a Plateau example also in the Burke. The flat bag suspended from the saddle's horn is painted after an old bag in the Holm collection, and both the saddle-bag (also called a drape) behind the rider and the collar about the horse's neck are also based on flat bags owned by the Holms. Horse collars of this type were often made by piecing together the parts from the two woven and decorated sides of existing flat bags.[24] In this case, the piecing together was done only in the painting, based on the designs taken off the Holms's original bags. The same approach was used to create the image of the saddle-bag.

Holm made an example of the indigenous style of beaded stirrup seen here: a bentwood frame covered with rawhide, and decorated in the patterns and colors typical of Plateau beadwork. The fully beaded strip on the red blanket about the woman's waist was made by Georg Barth, a German friend and fellow craftsman who occasionally visits the United States for research and inspiration.

Major institutions of the First Nations art field, in addition to the many individual collectors, make up an important segment of Holm's audience.[25] Dr. George MacDonald, former president of the Canadian Museum of Civilization Corporation in Hull, Quebec, elected to acquire *The Strike* (plate 37) for the collection of that prestigious museum. Holm had drawn a couple of smaller, related images, including the envelope sent to me in Neah Bay in 1978 (figure 7), and also a water-level view in charcoal and chalk, made as an illustration for one of the exhibit cases of Burke Museum artifacts that were on display in the Sea Monster House at the Pacific Science Center from 1972–1983. This latter picture accompanied a seal-skin float, harpoon-point, and harpoon line in the case, and depicted the side view of a canoe and a humpback whale at the same moment as portrayed in *The Strike*. The water view in the drawing was a cut-away, however, revealing the shape of the whale beneath the surface, which was longer and of larger girth than the vessel and crew closing in pursuit!

Holm's deep and enduring respect for the canoe builders, the whaling crews, and the whales—all together, as an interrelated phenomenon—has coalesced in this remarkable image. Long, slow rollers flow in from the open Pacific as the paddlers surge the canoe forward, led on by the graphically abstract spirit-of-the-canoe carved at the bow. The undulating curves of the painted Lightning Serpent echo the rhythm of the waves and the rippling knobs on the head of the whale. The faces of each crewman, and the dramatic geometry of the composition, combine to generate a great deal of power in the total image.

Holm felt satisfied that he was able in this canvas to depict so successfully the variegated nature of the clouds, and the hazy, misty effect of the shrouded shoreline, especially because they were completed in a one-shot sitting at his easel. He remains skeptical of his relative skills as a painter, but it is also clear that he values what he brings to his art—a special insight into the historical reality of the pictures. He feels also that his paintings give value and service to his audience, not as "fine art" or for their "painterly" qualities, but as *images* first and foremost. They are based on historical knowledge and on the personal experiences, real objects, and real events of his life; aspects that are imbued in the process, regardless of technique, and that bring to life the very real drama of their subjects.

Two of Holm's most recent pictures were painted for submission to the Settler's West "American Miniatures" show of 1996, held in their Tucson, Arizona, gallery: *Coup Counter* and *Buffalo Runner*. In *Coup Counter* (plate 38), the decoration on the man's body and the accouterments of his social position are drawn from Holm's studies of Crow warrior-society traditions. The shirt, hung with numerous hairlocks, is based on museum examples of the pipe-carriers' or war-party leader's style, and the moccasins are painted from photos of original examples. For the shield, Holm painted these designs on a matboard disk, attaching the appropriate tail feathers from the types of birds that often appear as war medicine. These tail feathers and the whole flicker skin were provided by examples from among the natural history specimens in the Burke Museum. The pipe-tomahawk is a recent one, which he modified from an inexpensive, cast-steel version that he brought at a gun and weapon show. A little filing here and there, the adding of typical cuts and stamped embellishments that weren't on the cast version, and letting it acquire a good rust patina made it into a presentable facsimile! The large and elaborately beaded drop attached to the beaded and tack-studded stem/handle is based on examples that are typical of certain northern Plains tomahawk drops. It is designed in one of Holm's favorite beadwork styles: that of the nineteenth-century Crow Nation, whose lands are near his boyhood home in southern Montana.

In *The Buffalo Runner* (plate 39), Holm wanted to depict a simple image with broad appeal and gave himself the exercise of representing this type of early-morning, back-lit scene. In this later work, we see less impressionistic handling of the clouds and color-patterns evident in the dawn sky than was apparent in the two paintings from the late 1950s (see figs. 1 and 2).

In contrast to the previous picture, the portrayal of *A Good Trade* (plate 40) is done in what Holm jokingly has referred to as his "*National Geographic* style." Every kind of imaginable scene is being played out in the context of the picture. The result is a rich, full image with a lot of cultural information present, and with more than an eyeful of spectacular fine-work to admire and inspect for detail. The large corn husk flat-bags containing the dried roots that are being offered in trade are painted from early-style examples either in the Burke Museum or on Holm's research slides.[26] The Plateau woman's hat and dress are similarly painted from the style of old pieces, as are the quill-wrapped horsehair shirt and beaded leggings of the mounted rider to her left. Examples similar to these are illustrated in *A Time of Gathering* (Wright, ed., 1991:6, 52, 53; figs. 8, 9). The bright red and green trade blanket was given to Holm by Jerrie Vanderhouen, a collector from Yakima, Washington, while the wide, spectacularly beaded blanket-strip on this robe is one made in "a good trade" for this painting by the German beadworker Georg Barth (and which also appears in *Yakama Sunset*, plate 36).[27] Crow styles of clothing and beadwork appear in the standing man's elaborate shirt (the figure is based on Barth and his work), the two wing-dresses of the Crow woman and her daughter, and the cradle board held by the young girl.

*The Last Chance* (plate 41) depicts one of the many energy-charged and exciting games of skill and intuitive power known to the Northwest Coast First Peoples. As avid players of this game, Holm and his family and guests have often passed many an evening hour in their fire or lamplit tipi on Goose Point, or at a beach encampment of the style in the painting. *S'lahal* (or *lehal*, as it is better known on the Canadian coast) is commonly called *bone game* in English or *stick game* east of the coast mountains, where it is played throughout the plains region. Tournaments and single extended games often draw out bets of thousands of dollars in "pot money." An earlier version of a related gambling game, called *lehallum*, was universal on the coast in the early nineteenth century. This game involved a number of small wooden disks, each differently marked, that were arranged by the team leader underneath a cloth. It was the challenge of the opposite team to guess the precise relationship of the disks to one another, using hand signals. Around the middle of the 1800s, the game depicted here had made its way to the coastal villages and was slowly supplanting the older pursuit.[28] This game brings out the most in its players in terms of intuition and ability to "see" in which hand the bone-shakers have hidden the female (unmarked) bone.

One of the most spirited games of s'lahal I ever attended was played between two full teams, one of men and one of women, the best two out of three, at a Makah Days celebration in Neah Bay, Washington. This game seesawed back and forth like the description in Holm's caption for this picture. It was down to one stick on this side, then down to one stick on the other, with parallel rises in the intensity of the singing and enthusiasm of the team members as well as the multitudinous observers to the contest. This game went on for a full *eight hours* before the final "last chance," the outcome of which carried the last counting-stick and the win to the men's team. The second game of the series was captured by the men in just four hours, to the dismay but not the discredit of the women's team players, who played hard and well and very nearly carried the game.

I had the pleasure of first learning this game in a late-night tipi party with the Holms on Goose Point (where the "stakes" were measured in cups of tea or cookies), and I have seen the enthusiasm and skill that Bill and Marty both exhibit for the game. On many of the canoe trips they have led through the San Juans, the game of s'lahal was known to echo through the late hours, providing Bill with a vivid mental and emotional picture of the beach, the fire and lamplight, and the spirit of the contest in action.

In this painting, the massive, organic curl of the stern of each of these huge canoes makes a backdrop for the scene played out on the beach. The singers tap out the lively gambling-song rhythms on a single round skin drum and with sticks on the driftwood logs at their knees. The glow of the fire and the oil-light splashes on the faces of the players, and the dark shadows retreat ever backward into the infinite calm and stillness of a quiet island night of a century ago. The pointer of the team on the right (whose signal hand is silhouetted against the yellow flames of the fire) has just lost his luck. He has indicated "both outside" with his fingers and thumb, but alas, the two bone-shakers of the singing team show up their hands with the two female bones both "inside." The last chance is gone. The winnings, the pile of Hudson's Bay trade blankets in the center of the game, will be carried away by the victorious team on the left of the picture.

The rhythm of Holm's painting life often seems to run in contrasting cycles of compositional style, alternating richly detailed and figure-filled scenes with more sparely composed examples, such as *The High Ridge* (plate 42). In the latter, the quiet solitude and the focused meditation of a transmontane hunter/scout is conveyed by the depth and the uncluttered nature of the painted scene. Holm had originally conceived this background as the setting for *Yakama Sunset*, but he decided the scene wasn't appropriate to that picture. John Putnam, the owner of this painting, has said that the area "looks like the Sawtooth Range in Idaho." The picture was named for the character of the location, which is not meant to be any particular place in the high Rockies. Among the objects that make up the scout's weapons and materials are several examples of Bill and Marty Holm's work, including the quirt made of Osage orange wood, the bear claw necklace, and the bow and arrow case, or quiver. Draped across the horse's neck is Marty's brown capote, changed to white for the context of this picture. The sitting for this picture was of course handled by SuperKen astride a simple frame, across which was draped the brown capote. The model wore or carried those accouterments at hand for the picture—quirt, quiver, shirt, etc.—and the drapery of the capote, with its tasseled hood hanging down at the horse's right shoulder, was set in this way just as it would appear in the painting.

A similarly uncluttered composition can be seen in the wide, panoramic format of *Sun Paints His Cheeks* (plate 43). Bill particularly likes this type of format, in part because "it's more like our normal vision." In addition, in this case at least, he already owned the frame (scouted previously at a secondhand shop for the purpose) and had stretched a canvas for it. Sun Dogs are a meteorological phenomenon in which Holm has always been interested, and the Native names for them reveal an especially beautiful kind of poetry. The title of *Sun Paints His Cheeks* comes from the Blackfeet tradition. The Sun Dogs that are the subject of this painting were photographed near the Swinomish Reservation in western Washington, while the Holms were on a sailboat trip heading south from Lopez Island. To begin with, the image was sketched with oil crayons. Holm then researched the proper appearance of the clouds for such an event, making and studying photographs of similar occurrences. In the final acrylic painting, however, the sky reverted to that in the original, imagined sketch. At one point, there was an additional horseman in the field of view, but he was painted out because the artist felt the composition was too cluttered. Holm says that he envisions the scene taking place "somewhere east of Great Falls, Montana." Through his eyes and hands, we see the spare vastness of the place and the moment, the casual reverence displayed by the congregated horsemen, and the image of the sun—his widely spaced cheeks painted with light—played against the variegated sky, all of which combine to create an image potent with timeless feeling and a quiet spirituality.

The distant subjects of *Sun Paints His Cheeks* are exchanged for an intimate, close-up portrait of a very special individual in a painting with a related astronomical title, *Sun, Moon, and Star* (plate 44). Here, as noted in Holm's text accompanying the picture, he has homed in on an old friend and admired elder, the wife of Kwakwaka'wakw artist and chief Mungo Martin (1884–1962). Her everyday name was Abayah (c. 1890–1963), and she and her husband taught the Holms a great deal. With an expression of radiant calm on her face, Abayah is displaying a string figure that illustrates the three celestial bodies of the title. The warm glow on her face looks as though it could be reflected from a fire, a kerosene lamp, or perhaps a dim electric light. The artist has focused in tightly upon the string figure and its maker, as if he is aware only of the fragile filament image and the patient personality of the one who is teaching its secrets to him. Abayah's rich personal history, obscured by the nondescript, mid-twentieth-century clothes she wears, is partly revealed in the imagery of the photographs on the wall behind her. The Weather Dance (her performance of which can be seen in one sequence of Edward Curtis's 1914 film *In the Land of the War Canoes*) is composed of an especially graceful, left and right spiral style of movement, something like the gathering of the sky before a storm, or the circular dance of the wind as it edges the clouds across the heavens. In the other photo, generations of Abayah's very traditional family pose behind her in her earliest years, a time when the Kwakwaka'wakw culture was fully rich and thriving. Holm has archival copies of these photos, and he thoroughly enjoyed reproducing them in this picture. The Sun, Moon, and Star was the first complex string figure that Bill and Marty learned from Abayah and Mungo, and one of a large number that they can still create. Many of Holm's friends have had the pleasure of seeing him hold forth with a series of these intriguing and enigmatic figures, reveling in the recitation of the stories or simple songs that accompany the string images.

This painting was done for a Sky World theme exhibit held at Seattle's Stonington Gallery in 1997. One of the aspects of this picture doesn't appear very clearly in a photographic reproduction — the string and the fingers and knuckles of Abayah are three-dimensional. To produce this subtle but remarkable effect, Holm first painted Abayah, basing her image on photographs, many of which he had taken himself. He then made the string figure, using a hard-laid commercial seine twine, which he treated with glue to stiffen it permanently. After gluing the stiffened string figure to the painting, he built up her fingers with epoxy filler, modeled in place on the canvas. These were then painted over to blend in with the rest of the image. He once had included a typically Kwakwaka'wakw type of small silver brooch at the neck of her dress, depicting a clasped pair of hands. The silver piece was of the kind made by his old acquaintance Dick Willy, a Tlatlasikwala traditionalist and silversmith to the old-timers. It proved distracting from the string figure, though, so he edited it out.

Holm's long-time friendship with Abayah and Mungo Martin and their extended families is also the foundation for *Welcome Dance* (plate 45). This view is the ceremonial opposite of *Approach to Tsakhees* (plate 18), though the location here is intended to be that of the beach at Yalis, the Kwakwala name for Alert Bay. Behind the sound of the chief's

24 / *Holm's life-size model, SuperKen, dressed as a Kwakwa̲ka'wakw Tł'asa̲la dancer.*
*Holm carved this fully articulated mannequin from redcedar, and included every major*
*body joint, right down to his fingers. Here SuperKen wears Bill's halibut button blanket, a*
*Kwakwa̲ka'wakw dancing apron with pendant coppers, and a frontlet and ermine headdress.*
*The frontlet was made by Bill in the Nuxalk (or Bella Coola) style. The raven rattle is one of*
*four made by Holm.*

dance-song and the lapping of the tiny swell on the gravel beach, one can almost hear the muffled thumps of the old paddle that taps against a canoe hull. The crews gently pull and push against the water to keep the canoes in line, and the vessels quite naturally tip slightly this way and that from minor imbalances within. These are the common traveling canoes of the nineteenth century, not painted with designs (as was the norm in that period), and showing off the graceful curves and flares that make them such a beautiful and seaworthy craft. The cloud of down wafting from the dancer's headdress, the percussive shake of deer hoofs or puffin bills on the dancer's apron, the tone and rhythm of the song—these are the more subtle, implied subjects of the painting, the parts that Holm's unique experience draws quietly into the scene. Summer after summer of reenacting such an event with his Kwakwaka'wakw guests has imprinted its intricacies on Holm's eye, enabling him to capture the essence of the moment.

Holm imagined the carved Sisiutl and Thunderbird headdress and the talking stick held by the nearest blanketed chief, though they are based loosely on similar-looking examples by historic Kwakwaka'wakw artists. The tree-design button blanket worn by the man on the right is painted after Marty Holm's own green and red blanket, which she has worn for countless occasions of traditional dancing. The man with the carved headdress wears a halibut-design blanket made by Holm many years back, and the other is a sort of composite, incorporating interesting traits from numerous examples. The large plaques of iridescent abalone shell seen here are not uncommon on older Kwakwaka'wakw regalia, traded from Pacific coastal beaches as distant as Mexico. Holm also has provided a touchstone or two within this picture, tying the historic imagery to the present time. Having seen such rare items on a few occasions while visiting Kwakwaka'wakw village sites, he painted in one small, blue Hudson's Bay faceted trade bead (in the lower left of the beach) and a copper wire bracelet on the lower right.

*Welcome Dance* was painted for and contributed to the auction fundraiser held in Campbell River to help rebuild the Alert Bay big-house, which had been destroyed by arson the previous year. (The picture was successfully bid for by Kodi Nelson, a young man renowned as an artist and a fine traditional dancer, who began performing with great spirit and uncanny expertise as a very young boy of elementary-school age.)

The subjects of Holm's paintings frequently reflect the kinds of coincidental influences and special events that arise in the larger framework of his ongoing studies. Such was the case with *Hidatsa Blackmouth Warrior* (plate 46). Several disparate paths converged to become this painting. A passionate quillworker, Holm had long admired and been inspired by the prodigious and persistent quillworking skills of the Hidatsa, who were close allies of the Mandan and whose historic territories include the upper Missouri country.

Holm conceived this image in part as a "show of quillwork styles." Certainly the finished product is that, with a variety of techniques and applications present. The multiple-quill plaited blanket strip with its quill-wrapped horsehair rosettes is the one that Holm made. The beautifully painted buffalo robe it decorates, however, is imaginary—based on known examples from the subject's time and region. The fantastically quilled shirt is a composite of several examples from the work of the Hidatsa, as is the spectacular split-horn bonnet. As he often does, Holm made up a canvas or soft cloth shirt or robe with the types of painted designs he wished to represent, modeling it on SuperKen in order to capture the proper drapery and folds that naturally come about in the wearing of such a garment.

Plains Indian pictographic records of war deeds often have information useful to the painter. That was the case in the planning of this painting. The most detailed of these pictographs were on paper, often on the pages of ledger books. These were made to be the account-recording instruments for the commerce of the time. Some of the traders and Indian agents in the early reservation period provided Plains artists with these bound ledgers for use as sketchbooks in which to note down those events the artists deemed worthy of commemoration. Innumerable ledger books contain the pictographic recount-ings of battles, historic events, and images of tipi-camp life that were rendered in land-scape format with graphite and colored pencil. Ledger books became quite common forms of pictographic art, and they survive as very important visual records of the times.

Pages of a ledger book in the collections of the National Museum of the American Indian show the exploits of a celebrated Hidatsa chief named Lean Wolf (also called Poor Wolf ). In one of the drawings Lean Wolf portrayed himself in war dress, carrying a so-called gunstock war club painted with diagonal stripes. An 1870 photograph by Stanley Morrow shows Lean Wolf holding a club of this type, painted with a striped de-sign. Lean Wolf was a member of the Hidatsa Blackmouth Society, one of whose em-blems was a curved wooden club with a blade inserted in the edge, probably referring to the gunstock type. The stripes on the club in the Lean Wolf pictographs and photo-graph, and his known membership in the Blackmouths, were the inspirations for the club in the painting. Holm had made a club of this type, with its characteristically lethal-looking iron stabbing-point, though his is decorated in an incised pictographic style. Modeled after that weapon for this picture, the Blackmouth warrior's club shows designs and a feather drop that were drawn for the picture from the decorations borne by the one in the ledger drawings.

Another area of particular interest and study for Holm has been the art styles of the cul-tural zones adjacent to the Tlingit/Northwest Coast–style culture area. Between the northwestern boundary of Tlingit cultural influence (the Yakutat/Controller Bay region) and the Yu'pik Eskimo country of southwestern Alaska lies a vast region, the territories of the Eyak, Chugach, Pacific Eskimo, and Aleut peoples (Alutiiq/Sugpiaq). Numerous artistic influences flow back and forth across these interrelated cultural boundaries — bowl types, headgear forms, and flat design styles. An important piece of Holm's scholarship in this field is an article that was published in the *Crossroads of Continents* exhibition catalog under the title, "Art and Culture Change at the Tlingit-Eskimo Border" (Fitzhugh and Crowell 1988).[29] In this chapter, Holm illustrated several examples of the type of woven spruce-root hat worn by the Alutiiq hunter in the painting of *Bird Skin Tunic* (plate 47) and described the relationship of their painted designs to examples from the Tlingit tradition. Related in form to the Tlingit/Northwest Coast spruce-root hats, these rare and visually impressive headpieces most often feature the rich embellishments of dentalia shells, beads, and sea lion whiskers seen on the example in this painting. Compared with Northwest Coast hats of the nineteenth century, the type seen here is generally of a more shallowly conical shape. Tlingit hats collected in the eighteenth century, the Northwest Coast contemporaries of the hat in this painting, are frequently less steeply flared in form than are their nineteenth-century counterparts. The characteristic Tlingit-style blue paint, derived from celadonite ore, here covers the surface of the hat, in bright contrast to the white of the dentalium shells.

As described in Holm's notes on the picture, the subject of this painting is dressed for the display of his finery, not for actual hunting, though he is posed with the weapons of his occupation. The bird skin tunic is based on examples collected by early explorers and collectors working with the Russian America Company, the aggressive fur-trading concern that was the first European influence in the region. One of the best collections of ethnographic material from this area was made by the then-chief manager of the Russian America Company, a man named Arvid Adolf Etholén (a Finnish national), who acquired some spectacular examples of this and other types of elaborate skin garments in the early nineteenth century (see Varjola 1990). Several of these exquisitely preserved examples toured with an exhibit of work from the Alutiiq/Sutpiaq and Northwest Coast areas, of which the bird skin garments were some of the most remarkable. Not many of these amazing garments have survived from the time period, and few others have been as well preserved as these — collected new, conveyed to Finnish and Russian museums, and packed away. Seldom displayed, they were thereby protected from the deleterious effects of excessive handling and exposure to light.

An extremely rare example of this type of hat came to public view, not too long before Holm created this painting, at an auction in California. Formerly the property of a small California museum, the hat was deaccessioned and sold on the open market, where it was successfully bid on by Dr. Allan Lobb, one of Seattle's well-known private collectors of basketry and Native arts (now deceased). Just how such an early and unusual Alaskan object came to be in California was naturally a subject of discussion at the time. Holm's hypothesis, which suggests one possibility, is that the hat's history may have included a connection to the Russian-America fur-trading outpost of Fort Ross, in northern California. Frequented by Russian-indentured Aleut and Alutiiq hunters, who harvested sea otter for the Russian America Company in the late eighteenth century, the fort may have been host to additional intercultural trade between the Alutiiq hunters and California Native Peoples, in whose possession the hat survived the better part of the last two centuries.

Holm's respect and admiration for such artistic handiwork motivates him to create images that incorporate the kinds of masterpieces of First Peoples art represented in this painting. His mind's eye has the ability to transport itself in time and place to be where individuals such as this hunter once lived, standing in contemplation of his world so different from our own. Museums can preserve and display a treasure, but the artist has the opportunity to breathe a new life into an artifact, returning the spirit that helped to bring it into existence, revealing the human aspects of life within its mantle, its protection and adornment. The unity of the world that spawned these objects—the hat, the tunic, the atlatl—is once again visibly manifested, at least in the miniature universe of the painted canvas, revitalizing the understated glory and dignity that were the context of their origin.

Similarly, the assemblage of artifacts in *The Spanish Broad Sword* (plate 48) is brought to life within the moment portrayed in the painting. The separate artifacts are in fact scattered about the world, carried here and there by the consequences of time and opportunity, each no longer a part of the others. They may not actually have all belonged to the same man, but the same hands took part in their creation, whether they were all of a piece or made for different individuals. The original artist's style of pictography is what unites the objects and in turn has motivated the painting, beautifully interpreted for us by Holm's visual style of scholarship.

This painting came about in part as the culmination of research for a lecture. Holm has been an annual participant in the Plains Indian Seminar, hosted by the Buffalo Bill Historical Center in Cody, Wyoming, since its inception in 1976, and he looks forward every year to participating with the symposium's assembled scholars and enthusiasts. For the 1998 Cody conference, he worked up a presentation on the pictography of what appears to be a single outstanding, though unnamed, probably Crow or Hidatsa artist.[30] To illustrate his presentation, he painted copies of several of the creations attributed to this artist. In *The Spanish Broad Sword* he has reunited a set of fantastically decorated garments that currently reside great distances from their places of origin, providing for them a living visual context. This unnamed man decked out in finery is representative of a special class of warriors or statesmen who, as admired leaders, were clad in the combined artistry of men and women who wished to honor with their handwork those who manifested the best of a nation's spirit.

Research by Holm and others has revealed that the earliest collection date for an object attributed to this particular artist is 1830, and the most recent date an example of his work was collected is 1905, although it was clearly made long before that time. The shirt and leggings in this painting were acquired in 1905 by a Czech nobleman, traveling in the American West, who presented the garments to the Opočno Castle Museum in what is now the Czech Republic. Other examples of the artist's work can be found in the National Museum of the American Indian, New York/Washington, D.C.; the National Museum of Denmark, Copenhagen; the Bern Historical Museum in Bern, Switzerland; at least one private collection in the United States; and a possible attribution at the National Museum of Natural History of the Smithsonian Institution.

Among the pictographic images in the original artist's compositions are many representations of weapons — such as lances with otter wraps, bows, muskets, etc. — each depicted in the traditional way, with adjacent "capture hands" indicating their means of acquisition. In addition to these expected kinds of weaponry, one sees a strange and not-easily-recognized design that went unidentified by many who studied the pictographs (and which appears in the painting below the man's left shoulder, just above the quilled blanket strip). No less than four of these enigmatic symbols can be seen among the pictographs on the shirt shown in this painting, none of which are directly associated with capture hand symbols. Holm's inquiring eye saw a possibility, and, on intuition, he looked into the various types and styles of swords that showed a resemblance to the drawings, and which may have been present on the northern Plains in the time period of the artist's life.

Books on swords, a trip to the Military Museum in Brussels (undertaken during a visit to his daughter Carla and her family), and consultation with various authorities all yielded welcome information. Probable confirmation was provided by the sword expert for Sotheby's, Ltd., who agreed that the pictographs resembled an early style of Spanish sword. Another scholar of Plains Indian material, Danek Mozdzenski, also recognized the probable identity of the painted designs and was able to corroborate the conclusions arrived at by Holm's work on the subject. The closest stylistic match to

25 / SuperKen dressed for the sitting of The Spanish Broad Sword (*plate 48*). *The flannel shirt is painted with the same pictographic images as the Opočno Castle Museum shirt. The representations of quilled and beaded shoulder strips are also painted designs, done on heavy canvas. The neckpiece was digitally scanned from a photo of the original shirt. Holm made the Crow-style hairpieces using dentalium shells, beads, feathers, and hairpipes based on early nineteenth-century original examples. The quilled strips on the eagle feathers used as hair decoration represent Holm's service record from World War II. The sculptured face of SuperKen is so naturalistic that it often startles people who come to the studio for the first time.*

26 / SuperKen wearing Holm's quill-wrapped horsehair shirt and Crow/Plateau-style breechclout, leggings, and moccasins.

the type of weapon represented in these early pictographs seems to be the seventeenth-century Spanish style of military broad sword. Though they are not accurately drawn to scale when compared with actual examples of such a sword, Holm has said that the pictographs representing the swords are, on the whole, "a more accurate rendering than those of the guns."

Possible means by which the sword might have arrived on the northern Great Plains are not difficult to imagine. These swords had remained in use in the Spanish American colonies far longer than in Europe, and some of them were likely captured in the course of early Native uprisings against Spanish rule. A sword of this very type, in fact, was discovered in recent years when it eroded out of a riverbank near Cochiti Pueblo in New Mexico. Horse breeding for the trade market was well developed in what is now the American Southwest by the late eighteenth century, and breeding animals were herded north and onto the plains by Comancheros, as traders from the then-Spanish-held territory were known. Along with the horses went bits, bridles, a variety of associated horse gear, and probably other accouterments of warfare.

While assembling the results of his research into *The Spanish Broad Sword*, Holm utilized a number of references relating to this pictographer's work.[31] To facilitate his work on the garments that appear in the painting, he made up a flannel shirt with all the pictographic designs as they appear on the original objects. He then created and fastened to it painted-canvas mockups of the decorative multiple-quill-plaited and beaded shoulder and sleeve strips of the shirt. He draped a tanned moosehide robe on the arm of SuperKen to model the natural folds and drapery of the buffalo robe in the painting, and he afterward painted in the appropriate pictographs. His own related Crow-style blanket strip was used to model the lay of that feature on the buffalo robe. Photographs of the shirt, leggings, and robe revealed the actual colors of the decorative pieces, as well as the deliberate asymmetry of the painted designs and geometric patterns on the quilled-and-beaded strips.

For the sword itself, he shaped a wooden handle, wrapped it with string and painted it a copper color to imitate the construction details of an original sword, and he fashioned a blade from a piece of thin aluminum sheet of flashing stock. Aluminum rods produced the curving bails and features of the characteristic grip guard. The eagle tail fan attached to the sword in the painting reflects the original decoration of the sword as it appears in the pictographs. The whole broad sword mock-up was far more detailed than was even remotely necessary to create its painted image, but Holm characteristically enjoys going to considerable extra effort in order to feel personally connected to the results of his work.

WAFTING EAGLE DOWN AND SOFT FIRELIGHT SET THE TONE in Holm's most recent painting *Hoylikạlat* (May 1999) (plate 49). In this dramatically composed picture, the Hoylikạlat dancer leans forward in the formal pose of the dance tradition, his raven rattle shaking steadily in his right hand, his left arm slightly raised in the regally magnanimous gesture that characterizes the dance. The Hoylikạlat is a Kwakwạka'wakw headdress dance that is the highest-ranking hereditary privilege of the Tlasulá, the traditional counterpart of the Winter Ceremonial. Some of the songs used for this performance are of asymmetrical rhythmic character, and require an expert dancer with a thorough knowledge of the twists and turns of the songs. Such rhythms challenge the performer to remain in time with the singers as one hops and turns about in the ritualized movements of the dance. The origin of the frontlet and headdress dance tradition was on the northern Northwest Coast among the Tsimshian, and the hereditary privilege spread north and southward through intermarriage and potlatch gifting, developing new regional variants along the way. The carved wooden frontlet-style headdress is the usual regalia for this performance, along with a decorated dancing robe, apron, and rattle. Among those Kwakwạka'wakw families with Tlingit ancestry, the woven Chilkat-style dancing blanket is used. It is the presence of the rattle and the typical postures of this dance, along with the specialized songs composed for the tradition, that distinguish it from other "peace" dances or headdress dances of the Kwakwạka'wakw.

The regalia worn by the young dancer in this picture (which was modeled by SuperKen) came from a combination of sources, both real and imaginary. The dancing robe or blanket, with its elaborate shell-button border designs, is painted from one that Holm made for himself in the 1950s. The nineteenth- or early twentieth-century dancing apron was acquired from from its Kwakiutl owner. The long, narrow apron is made of cloth with beaded design elements and is hung with puffin beaks as the rattle-makers. The twisted cedar bark neck ring is an imaginary original, based on historical examples, as are the headdress, frontlet, and raven rattle. This frontlet has the look of one made in the nineteenth century by a Kwakwạka'wakw carver, and includes unusually large pieces of blue-green abalone shell inlaid in the wide, reflective rim. The vertical filaments atop the headdress are sea lion whiskers, which restrain and filter the tufts of eagle down that are shaken out by the dancer's movements. The enclosing filaments were occasionally made of shaved-down strips of amber-colored whale baleen, like those on one of Holm's historical headdresses, and sometimes substituted for the very-hard-to-acquire whiskers. One piece of baleen (perhaps salvaged from a beached whale) would make dozens of filaments, while it would take the longest whiskers of ten or more very large sea lions to make up enough for one headdress. The raven rattle held by the dancer is based on historical rattles and the four or five that Holm had made in the last thirty years.

In this picture Holm has put the viewer right on the floor of the big-house—we are even closer than the audience would typically be. We see the performer as another dancer would, straight in the eye, as if the two are calculating their movements in relation to one another. Behind and to the left, the attendant (or dancer's helper) is cloaked in a folded trade blanket, watching the performance with care and admiration. In the right background, the shadowed forms of a massive housepost lurk on the edge of the firelight.

This post is carved in a Dzunuḵ'wa image—the Wild Woman of the Woods—rendered in a style of the early to middle nineteenth century. There is no white background or detail painting, and the sculpture is very rounded in form. The image appears more muted and naturalistic than is typical of the often stylized and abstract sculptural approaches and high-contrast painting styles of twentieth-century artists. The recessed narrow eyes, pursed lips, high cheekbones, and hollowed cheeks are the identifiers of the Dzunuḵ'wa image, against whose darkly blackened face the vermilion red of the lips, eyes, and cheeks fairly glows by the firelight. The Dzunuḵ'wa is depicted holding a large copper against her breast. The face of the copper is painted with an eagle or other bird design, in a style that also shows northern coast formline design. The copper is a cultural symbol of wealth, over which the Dzunuḵ'wa has traditional propriety. If a person sees or captures one of these creatures in the woods, he is said to obtain the Dzunuḵ'wa's great wealth. The copper is a cultural symbol of wealth, over which the Dzunuḵ'wa has traditional propriety. Her gaunt, shadowed face on the rim of this image speaks for the ancient ones, those who preceded the lives of human beings in this region, and who traverse today among us unseen by our busy and distracted eyes.

In his own words, Holm's paintings are often made to create scenes or images that "I'd rather be able to see in person." His vision sets out to capture people and places "as they would have appeared in color photographs done before the technology actually existed." He sees through a lens "as if a time-filter were on my camera," and he zooms back a hundred and fifty years or more to a time that was seldom otherwise documented, in a way that can speak directly to the inner eye of people living today.

The paintings of Bill Holm never cease to fascinate and inform his audience, and every new image is awaited by an enthusiastic group of followers. Though he is not prolific by the standards of artists for whom painting is their prime occupation, a steady stream of work flows from Holm's small but comfortable studio. Each painting, frequently the subject of fairly complex supportive research, may take weeks or months to complete, divided as his time is among various pursuits. He enjoys working out the details of each canvas and meeting its challenges. Each canvas is a window into a complex and ancient spirit, and each reveals as well something valuable about the painter himself and the worlds that are his guiding inspiration. To the many people who admire and respect the universe from which these images emerge, the work of Bill Holm is a welcome and cherished addition to their homes, their libraries, their lives, and their spirits.

# NOTES

1. George Hunt was the son of Scottish HBC factor Robert Hunt and his Tongass Tlingit wife, Anisalaga (whose English name was Mary Ebbetts). Hunt provided reams of transcribed information on material and ceremonial culture as well as hundreds of artifacts to anthropologist Franz Boas and others who co-published his work. He was the primary informant for Edward Curtis in 1914, as well as for Adrian Jacobsen earlier, and for the Milwaukee Public Museum's ethnologist Samuel Barrett. The canoe-making account is contained in Boas's *The Kwakiutl of Vancouver Island*, part of the Jesup Expedition Series of 1909, published by the American Museum of Natural History in New York. For additional information on canoe-making processes recorded by Hunt, see Boas's *Ethnology of the Kwakiutl*, the 35th Annual Report of the American Bureau of Ethnography, Washington, D.C., 1921.

2. When he painted *Kwakiutl Canoes* in 1959, Holm had not yet seen the surviving footage of Edward S. Curtis's silent motion picture, *In the Land of the Head-Hunters*, filmed among the Kwakwaka'wakw in 1914. Between 1967 and 1974, however, he became deeply involved in its restoration. The restored film, with a soundtrack added, was retitled *In the Land of the War Canoes* (see Holm and Quimby 1980). In 1967, he and his family traveled to Kwakwaka'wakw villages with a 16mm copy, showing the film and sharing with the villagers the excitement of its historic scenes, including many very dramatic shots of big canoes charging through the water. Several people among those in the audiences on this trip had taken part in making the film some fifty-three years earlier! This was the first time, however, that any of the Kwakwaka'wakw people had seen the results of their efforts, and their comments and sug-

gestions to Holm were especially useful to the restoration project.

3. Classes ceased to be held at Lincoln in 1982, when the school was officially closed. The building subsequently housed several small, community-based businesses. In 1997 the Seattle School District renovated it for use as an interim school facility while Ballard High School was being razed and rebuilt. The Holm painting is still intact.

4. The catalog is out of print at this time. Its scholarly articles address a wide range of subjects in the field of Alaska Native art and culture. Each of the articles is based, at least in part, on some object in the Sheldon Jackson collection, one of the most extensive in Alaska. The museum was founded in 1888 by the Reverend Sheldon Jackson along with the Sitka Training School, now a private college that bears his name. In 1982, the museum and its holdings of artifacts were purchased from Sheldon Jackson College by the State of Alaska, to become a member of the Alaska State Museums and a companion institution to the younger but well-established Alaska State Museum in Juneau.

5. This painting, along with *The Sea Otter Dart* (plate 21), was published in James Cassidy, editor, *Through Indian Eyes: The Untold Story of Native American Peoples* (1995).

6. "A Japanese junk was wrecked on the coast of Alaska near Sitka, and the men settled on an island opposite Sitka, which came to be called Japonski Island by the Russians. They returned to Edo [Tokyo] in 1806, either by the Russians or in a ship built from the wreckage. (Brooks; Davis)" (Plummer 1991:233).

7. Holms tells this story of the first time the Tulalip canoe was launched: Joe Gobin, one of the two carvers of the canoe, had injured his

back and was not able to paddle. He eventually took this position in the bow of the canoe, riding over the waves, emulating the man in the painting.

8. Coincidentally, a similar horse mask appeared on the artifact market in the early 1990s. It became part of the Eugene and Clare Thaw Collection of Native American Art, now housed at the Fenimore House Native American wing at the New York State Historical Association in Cooperstown, NY (T97). This mask, collected from a Nez Perce family at Nespelem, Washington, was unknown to Holm prior to the execution of this painting. The Nez Perce horse mask is illustrated in Vincent 1995:45.

9. A nineteenth-century example of this type of shirt is illustrated in the ATOG exhibit catalog (Wright, ed., 1991:52, fig. 8).

10. Holm has conducted more than one workshop and academic seminar on this technique for graduate-level and other students desiring such hands-on experience. His feelings about the value and importance of primary experience with processes and materials that are the subject of academic studies are contained in an unpublished paper, "Artifaking: Perception Enhancement by Doing," presented at the 1978 meeting of the American Anthropological Association held in Los Angeles. The making of this shirt also provided the background for his paper, "The Quill-Wrapped Horsehair Shirt," presented in 1987 at the Eleventh Annual Plains Indian Seminar, Buffalo Bill Historical Center, Cody, Wyoming.

11. Many such recently carved old guns have come onto the artifact market in various ways, though Holm says he knows of only two that are actually antique Northwest Coast pieces. One is also a shortened Northwest Trade Gun, carved in northern Northwest Coast style and housed in the UBC/MOA

(A1584). This was the original inspiration for Holm's artifake. The second is a brass barreled blunderbuss, originally the property of a Tlingit chieftain, that dates from the late eighteenth century. This short, large-caliber gun is beautifully carved on the stock and fore-end in an early northern coast style. It is now housed with the Eugene and Clare Thaw Collection of the New York State Historical Association, Cooperstown, New York (T210).

12. The bandoleer bag made by Mark Miller appears in *The Dandies* (plate 16), carried over the shoulder of the man on the left.

13. Such a bowcase-quiver is illustrated in ATOG (Wright, ed., 1991:63, fig. 18).

14. These two of the Northwest Trade Guns in Holm's collection were originally made as flintlocks, but were converted to percussion-cap style cocks (hammers) and nipples at some point in their history. Others were made as percussion-cap models to begin with, often well into the era of breech-loading and repeat-firing weapons. Something about the old muzzle-loading muskets and their specific design features has endeared them to the people who have traded for them throughout their history.

15. The Kwakwala name for the old-style dwelling and ceremonial structures is *walas gukw*, which literally translates to "big-house." In recent years, heavy rains and runoff (perhaps related to increased development in the general area) caused an unusually swollen stream to cut through the sand and gravel of the beach in a direct line to the waters of Beaver Harbour. Though the old-time big-houses are gone from this village, the gap between the beach and the foreshore, where the modern houses stand, is still dotted with smokehouses for the annual preservation of salmon, clams, and other Native foods.

16. In 1997 the private owner of the land on which the camp was situated (Sperry Penin-

sula on south Lopez) sold the land to ex-Microsoft billionaire Paul Allen, who acquired the property for his personal residence. The entity of Camp Nor'wester has since relocated within the San Juans, on Johns Island in the northwestern part of the archipelago.

17. Holm has a spruce-root woven hat made by Haida weaver Holly Churchill which also influenced the form of the one in the picture, but the hat's surface-painting is not yet completed at this writing. With Churchill's help in fine-splitting the roots, Holm is weaving a set of rings to be mounted on this hat.

18. For two decades and more, Vi Hilbert has taught Lushootseed, the language and literature of her ancestors, in schools and to tribal groups and in the American Indian Studies Program at the University of Washington. She has traveled nationwide as a storyteller and has been documented in film and video programs. Public television affiliate station KCTS in Seattle recently produced an hour-long documentary on the Lushootseed language and the efforts of Hilbert and other regional Native elders in a program entitled *Huchoosudah* ("everything that can be known"). The program is available through PBS.

19. In 1846, Paul Kane used his field watercolors to illustrate an elaborate mat-lodge shelter such as this from the Ft. Victoria area, only 25 sea miles from the site of the picture, as well as several scenes depicting the same style of canoe (Harper 1970: 254, fig. 184; 255, fig. 186; 261, fig. 196). Edward S. Curtis photographed numerous views of a temporary shelter of mats in the Skokomish River area, with a small canoe of this style and several baskets in evidence among the people in these pictures (Curtis 1913, plate 302).

20. See Steve Brown's essay on the ethnographic value of Paul Kane's work in *Nothing but a Passenger: The Field Notes and Water-*

*colors of Paul Kane*, edited by Ian MacLaren (Orange, Texas: Stark Museum of Art, forthcoming).

21. Determining one's longitude by use of a ship's chronometer (the precursor to the electronic methods of Loran and GPS) was a new technology at the time, only a few decades in existence. The instrument and its technique had been perfected in the 1760s by an obsessive and ingenious clockmaker, the Englishman John Harrison, after more than thirty years of design and prototype fabrication. A direct copy of the 1760 version of Harrison's chronometer (made by John Kendall) traveled with Captain James Cook on his second and third voyages of circumnavigation in the 1770s (Sobel 1995: 138–51). One of the more tried-and-true longitude methods of the time, however, absolutely depended on clear (cloud-free) observations from a solid-ground platform. This involved noting the time of the passage of one of Jupiter's moons as it was eclipsed by the face of the planet, and comparing the data with the information found in printed tables that recorded such observations from previous decades (known as *ephemerides*). Comparing the time difference of the data from the tables, and the timing of the data from the present observations, would enable the computation of the navigator's specific longitude. The four moons orbiting Jupiter are called the Galilean Satellites, in honor of Galileo Galilei, who pioneered the technique in the early 1600s (ibid.:26).

22. This painting by Mark Myers has been published in A. Hurst et al., *The Tall Ship in Art* (London: Wellington House, 1998: 119), and by the Alaska State Museum as the catalog cover and a poster for their 1994 exhibit: *Search for the Northwest Passage.*

23. Nuu-chah-nulth oral history also notes the observation of this Spanish ship by the

Hesquiaht people, whose territories lie about ten miles southeast of Yuquot, around the tip of Estevan Point. The event is embodied in their representation of the "First White Man," incorporated into the front of a *Hinkeets* mask tradition which is owned by the family of Chief Ben Andrews (Tim Paul, personal communication, 1994; see Brown 1995:264, fig. 99).

24. Two related pieces of this type are illustrated in Wright, ed., 1991:58, 59; figs. 13, 14.

25. The Alaska State Museum, for example, owns *Potlatch Guests Arriving at Sitka, Winter 1803* (plate 6).

26. The bag on the far left is painted from Burke Museum #2-1974, illustrated in Wright, ed., 1991:56, fig. 11.

27. Related examples can also be seen in Wright, ed., 1991:60, 61; figs. 15, 16.

28. The name of the newer game changes from *lehal* to s'*lahal* across the current international boundary, because the Straits and Lushootseed dialects of the Coast Salish language family add a nominal "s" to words used as nouns.

29. A related article by Holm, "Cultural Exchange Across the Gulf of Alaska: Eighteenth-Century Tlingit and Pacific Eskimo Art in Spain," was included in *Culturas de la Costa Noroeste de America* (Madrid: Museo de America, 1988). This study looks at the early Northwest Coast and Pacific Eskimo collections made by the Spanish explorers and discusses their relationships in forms and style.

30. The Crow/Hidatsa tribal attribution is conditionally agreed upon by many of the scholars who have researched the work of this artist, though Holm has stressed that there is currently *no* documentation that connects the man unequivocally with the Crow or Hidatsa Nations. The styles of bead and quill work associated with the pictographs are surely northern Plains, but the early quillwork techniques and designs were shared by a number of Plains Nations, and were not as differentiated as are the later beadwork styles of the post-1850s.

31. Very accurate reproductions of these pictographs were traced by Arni Brownstone from the actual garments, scanned, and used to illustrate his essay entitled "The Origins of Seven Hide Paintings," in the forthcoming anthology honoring the work of Norman Feder, edited by Christian Feest (Feest 2000).

# SOURCES

Brooks, Charles Wolcott

1964    *Japanese Wrecks Stranded and Picked Up Adrift in the North Pacific Ocean.* Originally
        published 1876 by the Academy of Sciences, San Francisco. Fairfield, Washington:
        Ye Galleon Press.

Brown, Steven C.

1995    *The Spirit Within: Northwest Coast Native Art from the John H. Hauberg
        Collection.* In association with the Seattle Art Museum. New York: Rizzoli.

1998    *Native Visions: Evolution in Northwest Coast Art from the Eighteenth through the
        Twentieth Century.* In association with the Seattle Art Museum. Seattle: University
        of Washington Press.

Cassidy, James J., editor

1995    *Through Indian Eyes: The Untold Story of Native American Peoples.* Pleasantville,
        New York: Reader's Digest Association.

Corey, Peter L., editor

1987    *Faces, Voices, and Dreams: A Celebration of the Centennial of the Sheldon Jackson
        Museum, 1888–1988.* Juneau: Division of Alaska State Museums and the Friends of
        the Alaska State Museum.

Curtis, Edward Sheriff

1913    *The North American Indian: Being a Series of Volumes Picturing and Describing the
        Indians of the United States, the Dominion of Canada, and Alaska.* Vol. 9. Frederick
        W. Hodge, editor. 20 vols. Norwood, Massachusetts: Plimpton Press. Reprinted 1970,
        Johnson Reprints.

Davis, Horace

1872    *Record of Japanese Vessels Driving upon the Northwest Coast of America and its
        Outlying Islands.* Worcester, Massachusetts: Charles Hamilton Palladium Office.

Emmons, George Thornton

1991    *The Tlingit Indians.* Edited with additions by Frederica de Laguna and a
        biography by Jean Low. Seattle: University of Washington Press/New York: American
        Museum of Natural History.

Feest, Christian, editor

2000    *Studies in North American Indian Art: A Memorial Tribute to Norman Feder.* Euro-
        pean Review of Native American Studies Monograph 2. Altenstadt 2000.

Fitzhugh, William W., and Aron Crowell, editors

1988    *Crossroads of Continents: Cultures of Siberia and Alaska.* Washington, D.C.:
        Smithsonian Institution.

Harper, J. Russell

1970    *Paul Kane's Frontier.* Fort Worth, Texas: Amon Carter Museum.

Plummer, Katherine

1991    *The Shogun's Reluctant Ambassadors: Japanese Sea Drifters in the North Pacific.*
        Portland: Oregon Historical Society.

Samuel, Cheryl

1987    *The Raven's Tail.* Vancouver: University of British Columbia Press.

Sobel, Dava

1995    *Longitude: The True Story of a Lone Genius Who Solved the Greatest Scientific
        Problem of His Time.* New York: Walker and Company.

Vancouver, George

1801    A *Voyage of Discovery to the North Pacific Ocean, and Round the World.*
        London: John Stockdale.

Varjola, Pirjo

1990    *The Etholén Collection: The ethnographic collection of Adolf Etholén and his contem-
        poraries in the National Museum of Finland.* Helsinki: National Board of Antiquities.

Vincent, Gilbert T.

1995    *Masterpieces of American Indian Art from the Eugene and Clare Thaw Collection.*
        In association with the New York State Historical Association. New York: Harry N.
        Abrams.

Waterman, Thomas T.

1920    *Whaling Equipment of the Makah Indians.* Seattle: University of Washington
        Publications.

Wright, Robin K., editor

1991    A *Time of Gathering· Native Heritage in Washington State.* Thomas Burke Memorial
        Washington State Museum. Monograph No. 7. Seattle: University of Washington
        Press.

Bill Holm © 1992

*Color Plates*

## 1 / NEZ PERCE SCOUT

*Oil on canvas board.* 18" × 24" (1955). *Collection of* The Western Horseman

*The Western Horseman.* August 1956. Cover

*Appaloosa News.* November 1961. Cover

*The Western Horseman Calendar.* 1966

A NEZ PERCE SCOUT, MOUNTED ON AN APPALOOSA HORSE, SURVEYS THE back trail during the flight across Montana in 1877. In the distance are the Bull Mountains, a range of rough sandstone bluffs covered with pines, just south of the Musselshell River. The Nez Perce have once more escaped the pursuing United States Army forces at the Battle of Canyon Creek on September 11, 1877, near present-day Laurel, Montana, and are moving northward toward their goal of crossing the Canadian border.

The scout wears trade cloth leggings and a blanket capote. He is armed with a bow and arrows and an 1873 Springfield carbine. Looking eastward, he is unaware that far over the horizon Colonel Nelson Miles is leading his troops across country to intercept the fleeing Nez Perce at Snake Creek, only forty miles from safety in Canada.

Just over the Bull Mountains to the north is present-day Roundup, Montana, where I was born and spent my boyhood.

## 2 / CROW TRAILING HORSES

*Casein on illustration board.* 20" × 20" (1957). *Collection of* The Western Horseman
*The Western Horseman.* June 1958. Cover

A CROW WARRIOR CARRIES A QUIRT AND A WINCHESTER MODEL 1866
carbine as he examines the tracks of a band of horses. The braided rawhide lariat over his
shoulder suggests that he is planning to come back with one or more of them. His own
dapple-gray is bareback and without a bridle. Only a thong is hitched around the pony's jaw,
with the long end run through a ring at the other end of the thong. The thong serves as reins,
with its trailing end coiled and tucked in the rider's belt. It comes free from his belt if he is
unhorsed, allowing him to catch his pony and remount.

    The lack of a blanket, leggings, or any provisions suggests that the horse trailer is not
expecting a long pursuit!

## 3 / KWAKIUTL CANOES

*Oil on canvas board.* 30" × 24" (1959). *Collection of Donn Charnley*
*The Beaver: Magazine of the North.* Summer 1961. Cover
*The Canoe.* 1983. Full-page, color
*Alaskafest.* May 1984. Alaska Airlines Magazine. Cover

THE PAINTING DEPICTS A KWAKIUTL CANOE TRAVELING DOWN KINGCOME Inlet near the mouth of Wakeman Sound sometime in the mid-nineteenth century. Another canoe is seen some distance away. The *Sisiutl*, a legendary serpentlike creature, is painted on the near canoe. The bowman wears a white Hudson's Bay Company blanket around his waist, but some of the crewmen are wearing cedar bark robes, suggesting that it is early in the trade period.

In 1958 I carved a 24-foot canoe, following the methods set forth in a detailed account of canoe-making recorded fifty years earlier by George Hunt and published by Franz Boas. I wrote an article on my canoe carving which was published with accompanying photographs in *The Beaver*, the Hudson's Bay Company magazine.

## 4 / VANCOUVER'S SHIP DISCOVERY AT RESTORATION POINT, MAY 1792

*Acrylic on canvas. 5′ × 30′ (1966). Lincoln High School Library, Seattle Public Schools*

ON MAY 19TH, 1792, THE SHIP *DISCOVERY*, UNDER THE COMMAND OF Captain George Vancouver, came to anchor off a point of land opposite the site of present-day Seattle, Washington. Vancouver's voyage to the Northwest Coast was for the twofold purpose of making an accurate survey of the coast and determining once and for all whether there existed a fabled Northwest Passage to the Atlantic, and to take over from Spain the settlement at Nootka Sound, which had been assigned to England in 1790. In the course of the survey, his ships *Discovery* and *Chatham* became the first European vessels to enter the system of waterways now known as Puget Sound. Vancouver chose the name Restoration Point to honor the anniversary of the restoration of the English monarchy.

The *Discovery* lay at anchor near Restoration Point until May 30, during which time boat parties surveyed the southern reaches of the Sound. The ship was visited by local Indians, who were camped on the point harvesting roots, and Vancouver visited the village as well. Vancouver's detailed description of this village and its inhabitants in his journal are the earliest written record of the Native peoples of the Seattle area. The later prominent chief, *Si'al* (Seattle), who was a small boy at the time, is thought to have been present in this village during Vancouver's visit.

## 5 / NORTHERN INDIANS TAKING A BREAK WHILE WAITING FOR THE WIND, CROSSING JUAN DE FUCA STRAIT ON THE WAY TO PUYALLUP TO PICK HOPS

*Serigraph, edition of 75. 11" × 20" (1984).*

*Print given to the participants in the raising of the frontal pole for my studio*

IN THE LATE NINETEENTH CENTURY THE HOP GROWING INDUSTRY burgeoned in the Puget Sound country, and large numbers of local Indians found paying labor in the hop fields. The demand for pickers was great enough to encourage Indians from far up the coast to travel in their big canoes to Puget Sound and join the work force. Long accustomed to the journey from earlier war and slave raids and trips to the Hudson's Bay Company's trading posts, the northern people considered the trip to be a relatively natural one. The voyage was leisurely, and advantage was taken of tide and wind. The longest crossing for many was the twenty-mile stretch from the San Juan Islands across to Admiralty Inlet at Port Townsend. Although sometimes stormy, the weather in the picking season was often characterized by flat calms.

Indians were amenable to hop picking. Work for cash was not easy to find, and hop picking filled that need. The seasonal character of the work fit in with their accustomed round of gathering, and the social atmosphere gave an almost festival air to the hop camps.

Here the wind has died for two big canoes from the north. The travelers rest awhile in hopes that it will spring up again. If not, the paddles will come out, and they will again be on their way.

## 6 / POTLATCH GUESTS ARRIVING AT SITKA, WINTER 1803

*Acrylic on canvas. 24" × 40" (1987). Collection of the Alaska State Museums*
*Friends of the Sheldon Jackson Museum poster. 1987*
*Faces, Voices, and Dreams.* Alaska State Museums. 1987. Double page, color
*Materials for the Study of Social Symbolism in Ancient and Tribal Art.* 1988
*Through Indian Eyes.* 1995. Double page, color.

THIS PAINTING ILLUSTRATED MY ARTICLE "THE HEAD CANOE" FOR THE Sheldon Jackson Museum's centennial volume, *Faces, Voices, and Dreams.* I wanted to show three canoe styles: the head canoe, the early form of the classic "northern" canoe that superseded the head canoe in the first decades of the nineteenth century, and the northern Tlingit "spruce" canoe that was related in form to the head canoe and continued in use until the twentieth century. The setting shown is the beach in front of the Sitka village, so the time had to be before the Russian trader Aleksandr Baranof drove the Tlingits from this site in 1804. When they returned to Sitka in 1821, the head canoe had gone out of use. Since the early form of the northern canoe was just being developed at the beginning of the century, I chose 1803 as the date of the picture. At that time the classic Chilkat blanket was just on the verge of appearing, so all the twined blankets in the picture are of the early geometric "Raven's Tail" form or the transitional design. The Tlingits had trade relations with Europeans for nearly a decade by that time, so trade blankets and European shirts would have been seen among them.

It is a clear winter morning, with the sun low in the south and Mount Edgecumbe looming over Japonski Island to the west. The host chief, in the shadow of the houses above the beach, greets his guests, who are dancing and singing in their canoes clustered in the channel just offshore.

# 7 / SPRING HUNT

*Acrylic on canvas. 24" × 36" (1987). Collection of Mr. and Mrs. Charles Butler*

A PLATEAU HUNTER RIDES THROUGH THE SAGEBRUSH ON A MORNING IN early spring, sometime in the 1860s or seventies. He wears trade cloth leggings and a capote or hooded coat made of a Hudson's Bay Company blanket. A green Hudson's Bay Company blanket is wrapped around his waist. Across his lap he carries a .56 caliber Leman percussion trade rifle, and his powder horn and bullet pouch hang from straps over his shoulder. From his wrist swings an elk antler–handled quirt with an otter skin strap. His saddle is man's style, with low pommel and cantle of antler covered with rawhide and padded with a piece of tanned buffalo hide. The stirrups are also Native-made of bentwood and rawhide.

The scene is just north of the big bend of the Columbia River, with the Horse Heaven Hills in the distant background.

## 8 / GOING VISITING

*Acrylic on canvas. 24" × 36" (1988). Collection of Tom and Roxana Augusztiny*

WESTERN WASHINGTON TRAVELING CANOES, ON THE WAY TO A POTLATCH, race over the waves before a November southwest wind at the turn of the century. The travelers relax and enjoy the ride, now passing through a welcome patch of afternoon sun. Only the steersman strains to keep the driving canoe off the wind. All the passengers are dressed in European fashion, typical of the period. The only visible example of traditional Native dress is the cedar bark hat worn by one woman.

Nineteenth-century Northwest Coast canoe sails were of canvas, sprit-rigged in imitation of the ships' boats of the early contact period. Many early explorers in their journals mention making sails for the Indians they encountered and describe teaching the canoemen to use them. Earlier Native sails were probably square-rigged cedar bark mats that were used only in running before the wind. The newer design enabled canoes to sail with the wind on the beam as well. Most Northwest Coast canoes of moderate size or larger were fitted with sails after European contact. The "Westcoast" or "Nootkan" style of canoe, seen here, was a very seaworthy craft and popular from the Columbia River to the north end of Vancouver Island as a traveling canoe.

## 9 / PARADE

*Acrylic on canvas.* 24" × 36" (1988). *Collection of Ray Snyder*

A NEZ PERCE WOMAN AND MAN IN THEIR FINEST DRESS AND HORSE GEAR
ride in the sun and dust to a celebration in the late nineteenth century. Many of the items
are family heirlooms, dating back many decades. The woman's dress of softly tanned mountain sheep skins, heavily embroidered with pony beads, is of the style of the mid-century.
Some of these very early dresses are still in use among Plateau people. Her horse's headstall
and its hand-forged Mexican bit are of the same period, as are her companion's pony-beaded
shirt and leggings, with their long, porcupine quill–wrapped fringes.

A pair of large, tapered cylindrical cases of painted rawhide with trailing fringes of heavy
buckskin, sometimes called warbonnet cases, hang on the sides of the woman's parade horse,
over a thickly fringed and beaded double saddle-bag. Her blanket strip and saddle are of a
style made also by the Crows and may have been traded from them. Plateau people, however,
had these in profusion and probably made many of them, as well as elaborate horse collars
of the Crow type. This one is a distinctively Plateau variant on that style. The woman's pony-
bead dress and basketry hat are uniquely Plateau.

Although also seen on the northern Plains, the striking horse mask of beaded trade cloth
and feathers was a more frequent sight on festive occasions on the Plateau. Eagle feather
warbonnets of the Plains type were also worn by Plateau warriors in the nineteenth century.
Many of them were of the upright type like this one, with broad browbands of simple design
and a profusion of dyed hackle feathers and ermine fringes.

## 10 / BEACH HARVEST, PUGET SOUND

*Acrylic on canvas. 24" × 36" (1988). Collection of Karen Holm*

A YOUNG SALISH WOMAN RESTS FOR A MOMENT AFTER AN AFTERNOON OF hard digging for clams near present-day Richmond Beach on Puget Sound. Her flattened forehead and cedar bark skirt indicate that the scene is no later than the early historic period, since European dress was widely adopted in the region by the middle of the nineteenth century. Although working at a common task, this is a woman of means, as shown by her copper bracelets and dentalium shell ear pendants. Her yew-wood digging stick has unearthed nearly a canoe load of clams, which she carries in an openwork basket of cedar root to her graceful little cedar craft. Light and fast, and easily managed by one or two paddlers, Salish canoes like this one were ideally suited for the relatively sheltered waters of the channels and islands of the sound, but in the hands of experienced paddlers they were seaworthy enough to handle rougher conditions. Paddle, cedar bark bailer, and cattail mat complete her traveling gear.

Across the sound, over present-day Point Jefferson and silhouetted against the foothills of the Olympic Mountains, can be seen the faint, drifting smoke from the Suquamish village on Agate Pass. Glaucous-winged gulls gather to search for scraps when the clam digger slides her canoe into the surf and paddles for home.

## 11 / ATE HE YE LO — SO SAYS THE FATHER

*Pencil on illustration board.* 18" × 24" (1990). *Collection of Duane Pasco*
Prix Dakota II Exhibition, High Plains Heritage Center. 1990
Traveled throughout South Dakota, 1990–91

"ATE HE YE LO, SO SAYS THE FATHER," WAS A PHRASE FREQUENTLY HEARD
in the Ghost Dance songs of the Lakota. Here three figures, part of a large circle of dancers,
appear as they might have been seen by an observer outside the circle. All wear muslin Ghost
Dance dress, painted with holy symbols and hung with eagle and magpie feathers. The man
in the center carries a Ghost Dance shield on his back.

The Ghost Dance began in Nevada in the 1870s as a response to the loss of land and culture to the tide of white immigration and government suppression. The founder taught that
its practice would return the land and the buffalo and remove the intruders. It quickly spread
across the Plains and, although the founder's teaching was pacifistic, settlers in the Dakotas
and Nebraska viewed it as a threat. In a tragic finale, over 200 Lakota and sixty soldiers were
killed or wounded at Wounded Knee, South Dakota on December 29, 1890. The Prix Dakota
exhibition, for which I made this drawing, was a centennial observance of that somber event.

Ate he yelo – So saith the Father                                    Bill Holm  © 1990

## 12 / SPONTOON TOMAHAWK

*Acrylic on board.* 48" × 30" (1989).

IN AN EASTERN PLATEAU TULE-MAT LONGHOUSE, A PROMINENT MAN speaks in council about the accomplishments of his grandfather, whose old-time spontoon tomahawk he carries. Although the tomahawk is a trade piece from the beginning of the nineteenth century, the setting here is about 1870. The speaker wears an ermine-trimmed bonnet with wooden, tack-studded horns. His fringed shirt is of an early style, with shoulder and sleeve strips of quill-wrapped horsehair. Panel leggings with beaded strips in the trans-montane style, pony-beaded moccasins, and a plaid woolen breechclout complete his dress. The listeners, seated on tule mats and robes, are dressed in Plateau style of the latter part of the century.

   This spontoon tomahawk is based on one in the Burke Museum of Natural History and Culture, collected near the Dalles on the Columbia River. Lewis and Clark described and illustrated tomahawks of this kind, which the expedition blacksmith made in large numbers for the Indians who visited the explorers' winter camp at Fort Mandan on the Missouri River. The tomahawks were in great demand, and their trade was an important source of corn for the expedition members. The journals speak disparagingly of the battle axes: "The length of the blade compared with the shortness of the handle render it a weapon of very little strength, particularly as it is always used on horseback: there is still however another form which is even worse, the same sort of handle being fixed to a blade resembling an espontoon."

## 13 / THE FLANKERS

*Acrylic on board.* 12" × 54" (1989). *Collection of Daphne Morris*

LAKOTA MEN, EQUIPPED FOR BATTLE, SCOUT THE RIDGES FLANKING THEIR moving village. Both are armed with muzzle-loading trade guns. One has the skin of a bird tied in his hair, while the other wears a long-trailed eagle feather warbonnet. Their faces are painted with protective, dreamed designs. One man wears war medicine and an eagle bone whistle suspended from his neck. Bullet pouches and powder horns complete their equipment.

Plains Indian villages on the move were vulnerable to attack by enemy warriors, so members of the warrior societies rode far to the front and sides of the column, on the watch to discover and intercept any such danger.

Bill Holm © 1989

## 14 / PURIFYING THE SHIELD

*Acrylic on canvas.* 36" × 24" (1990). *Collection of Mark Miller*

IN THE MID-NINETEENTH CENTURY, FIVE CROW MEN GATHER IN A TIPI TO ritually purify a shield in preparation for a war party. A smudge was made by burning incense —sweetgrass, juniper leaves, or some other sacred plant—and the shield, uncovered, was held in the smoke. Among Plains people, objects used ceremonially that were powerful or associated with power were consecrated by "smudging" in a sacred incense before their use. The incense material itself was usually sprinkled on a lighted buffalo chip placed on a ritually prepared altar space.

The ritual leader, with his pipe, wears a fringed war shirt decorated with strips of quill-wrapped horsehair. The other men are dressed and painted according to their war medicines. The trailing headdress of hair spotted with painted pitch, worn here by the shield owner, was so popular with nineteenth-century Crows and their Hidatsa relatives that it became a recognition sign for them, as is seen in the pictographs on the tipi lining. One warrior wears his hair tied on top of his head along with his war medicine of the stuffed skin of a male kestrel. Another carries his split-horn warbonnet slung on his back, and he cradles a flintlock trade musket across his lap.

## 15 / THE DECISION

*Acrylic on canvas.* 30" × 48" (1990). *Collection of Mark Miller*

ON THE MORNING OF JUNE 25, 1876, GENERAL GEORGE ARMSTRONG CUSTER joined a group of his Crow Indian scouts on a high point in the Wolf Mountains in southeastern Montana. He was trying to see the Sioux and Cheyenne village the scouts had discovered just after dawn. Apparently visibility had decreased as the morning grew warmer, and Custer was unable to see the signs of the village that his scouts attempted to point out to him. He accepted their insistence that the village lay in the Little Bighorn valley just over fifteen miles away. Since there were indications that Custer's column had been discovered by the enemy, he made the fateful decision to attack the village at once. There were more than a dozen people on the ridge at the time, but I have shown only Custer, three of the Crow scouts (White Swan with his telescope, Whiteman Runs Him, and Goes Ahead), Lieutenant Charles Varnum (chief of Custer's Indian scout detachment), and the civilian scout Charley Reynolds. The scene is based on the actual appearance of the terrain, from as nearly the correct spot as I could find and in nearly the identical season and atmospheric conditions.

## 16 / THE DANDIES

*Acrylic on canvas. 26" × 44" (1990). Collection of David and Ann Eschenbach*

TWO YOUNG MEN, DRESSED IN THEIR FINEST, SURVEY THEIR CROW CAMP from the edge of a rimrock overlooking the river valley. They are about to cruise the camp, and their elaborate regalia, paint, and fine horses are intended to impress the young women. One wears a richly decorated otter skin bowcase-quiver and carries a love medicine in the form of a bull elk cut out of rawhide. From his ankles hang complex pendants of skunk skin, red trade cloth, beads, quillwork, and fringe. His companion's trade gun is cased in a beaded and fringed scabbard, and rather than an everyday, functional bullet pouch, he wears an elaborate bandoleer bag. Ornaments of dentalium shell and hair pipes, topped with fancy feathers, flank their carefully dressed and painted hair. Both wear beaded panel leggings of blue blanket and red trade cloth. The scene is set in an early evening of the 1870s, looking eastward toward the distant mountains.

## 17 / RAVEN WARRIOR

*Acrylic on canvas.* 36" × 24" (1991). *Collection of Lloyd Averill*
*American Indian Art Magazine.* Winter 1993

SCREENED BY THE FOG, A TLINGIT WAR PARTY IN THE EARLY NINETEENTH century approaches an enemy village. The warriors paddle silently, steering their great war canoes close to the steep shore. The canoes are the ancient battle craft, with upright, broad, and flaring bows, apparently designed as a shield against arrows. These high bows are said to have been removable for ease in traveling. Their details seem to be exaggerations of classic Nootkan canoe design, but these war canoes were used in the early historic period all along the coast, from Vancouver Island to Alaska. They are known today only from a few drawings and paintings and a handful of Native models. The Tlingit name of this canoe type was *kookh-da-gi-gin-yakw.* The Kwakiutl term was *muhnka,* and it is by this name that the archaic canoe is best known today. The U'mista spelling is *ma̱nk̲a.*

Standing in the bow of the lead canoe is a warrior armed with a flintlock trade musket and steel dagger, the pommel of which is in the form of a raven's head. Raven's image, a crest derived from lineage myths, appears on his canoe and paddles, his heavy hide armor, and his carved helmet with its trailing plume of human hair. All the warriors are armed with daggers or spears, and all wear armor, some of it reinforced with rows of Chinese coins.

Above the canoes, a pair of ravens wheel and call in the fog. They are nature's counterparts of the mythical culture hero, Raven, the source of the images below. All along the Northwest Coast there was the belief that ravens spoke a language that could be understood by those given that power. Ravens could foretell victory or danger. Perhaps these are off to tell the unsuspecting village of the warriors' approach.

## 18 / APPROACH TO TSAKHEES, 1890

*Acrylic on canvas.* 24" × 36" (1991). *Collection of Loren Smith*
*De Facto Art Magazine.* 1999 (20).


AFTER MONTHS OF PREPARATION, A KWAKIUTL CHIEF IS READY TO BRING
out in a lavish potlatch the noble prerogatives that are being passed on to his children. In
order to properly validate those privileges, he has invited the people of other villages to act
as witnesses. As the invited guests arrive, they assemble their canoes in the winter afternoon
light off the shelving beach of the village of Tsakhees ("Water running on the beach," named
for the little stream that runs along the base of the bank). While the paddlers sing and beat
time on the gunwales of the canoes with their paddles, a dancer wearing the elaborately embellished dancing headdress performs in the bow of the lead canoe, scattering eagle down,
signifying peace, from his crown of sea lion whiskers. The villagers gather on the beach and
on the bank in front of the big, plank houses. The house chief and his speaker prepare to welcome the visitors, while on the beach, singers and headdress dancers stand ready to perform a
welcoming dance in response to that of their guests.

The village of Tsakhees stood close by the Hudson's Bay Company's trading post of Fort
Rupert, on the shore of Beaver Harbour on Vancouver Island's north coast. Although the
owners of many of these houses owned the privilege of painted house fronts, none of these
particular houses had painted fronts, according to photographs of the period. Tsakhees, or
Fort Rupert as it is known in English, is still a thriving community today.

## 19 / THE INVITER

*Acrylic on linen.* 16" × 12" (1992). *Collection of Bruce and Linda Colasurdo*

A TLINGIT VILLAGE CHIEF WATCHES THE APPROACH OF HIS INVITED guests arriving by canoe. He is the custodian of noble emblems, the clan crests that attest to the aristocracy of his lineage. Primary among these is a painted spruce root hat, topped with a column of basketry cylinders supporting the carved figure of the fin of the killer whale. The hat painting depicts the whale itself, blowhole represented by a human face with its body streaming back as the whale's breath. Clan crest hats are the royal crowns of Tlingit nobility, to be worn only on occasions of the greatest importance. In this way, the inviter honors his guests.

Over the chief's shoulders drapes a Chilkat robe. Even more abstractly stylized than the painting on the hat, a diving killer whale in broad, black formlines, enriched with yellow and blue detail, spreads across the back of the robe and over the wearer's shoulders. Dancing nobles all along the coast carry rattles shaped as a raven bearing a mysterious assemblage of figures on its back. The inviter will dance on the shore in response to the ceremonial arrival of the visitors. A rich finishing touch to his noble dress are the great shark-tooth earrings, said to have been worn only by chiefs.

## 20 / HAMSAMALA

*Acrylic on canvas.* 30" × 24" (1992). *Collection of Tom and Jackie Bernard*
*De Facto Art Magazine.* 1999 (20).

THE CANNIBAL DANCER, *HAMAT´SA*, HAS BEEN LURED BACK TO HIS VILLAGE
from the house of his motivating spirit. There the assembled tribes have partially tamed him,
but a phrase in his song has brought back his wildness, and he has dragged his encircling attendants around the floor and out behind the painted curtains at the back of the ceremonial
house. A great beak is heard to snap. Then, one by one, masked dancers—*Hamsamala*—
each accompanied by an attendant, step into the firelight. The Hamsamala represent the associates of the Man-Eating-Spirit. They dance upright at the corners of the floor, then drop
to jump squatting and turning, finally sitting on the ground, their great beaks swinging and
shuddering. A woman with taming power, shaking a round rattle, sings to calm the wildness
of the dancers. The dancers rise shouting, snap their beaks, and move to the next corners.
Only when the last Hamsamala has disappeared does the Hamat'sa reappear, and eventually
his taming is completed.

The Hamat'sa is the most prestigious of the Winter Ceremonial dances of the
Kwakwaka'wakw people of the northern Vancouver Island area. The masks used in the
taming of the Hamat'sa are among the most flamboyant in all of the Northwest Coast art.
Those seen here are the work of the master artist Willie Seaweed. The carver is shown
standing among the singers, enjoying his works in action. The setting is the Gwa'yasdam's
village Raven House of Chief John Scow, the carved posts of which are now in the
Seattle Art Museum.

## 21 / THE SEA OTTER DART

*Acrylic on canvas. 24" × 40" (1992). Collection of J. C. Chapman*

*Through Indian Eyes.* 1995

THE PEOPLE OF THE ALEUTIAN ISLANDS, THE ALASKA PENINSULA, KODIAK Island, and Prince William Sound were famous as sea hunters, paddling their narrow, skin-covered baidarkas fearlessly in the uncertain seas and weather of their world in pursuit of sea lions, seals, and sea otters. It was their skills in hunting sea otters that led to their early subjugation and eventual acculturation by Russian fur traders. Sea otter hunting required not only skill in maneuvering the slender baidarka, but accuracy with the throwing board and harpoon dart, surely one of the most elegantly designed hunting-weapon systems in history. In the easily capsized baidarka, the throwing board was a more efficient launching implement than the bow, since it required only one hand for its use, while the other hand held a steadying paddle. The dart was a marvel of design, with its slender, tapered wooden shaft and its elegantly constricted bone foreshaft. A small, barbed bone or copper point was held in a wooden socket set into the foreshaft, and was attached to the dart itself by a slender, Y-shaped bridle of finely braided sinew. When readied for use, the bridle was tightly wound onto the shaft. When the dart struck, the point came free and the bridle unwound, pulling the shaft vertically through the water, as a drag. When the otter surfaced, the feathered end of the shaft floated upright, marking the otter's location for the hunters.

High-ranking Aleut sea hunters wore prestigious bentwood hats, elaborately painted and lavishly decorated with carved ivory panels set with the long whiskers of Steller sea lions. The whiskers were ornamented with trade beads and feathers. Although it has been suggested that these hats were reserved to whalers, there is good evidence in early drawings, photographs, and models that they were also worn for hunting smaller sea mammals. Several types of bentwood visors were worn, as seen on the hunter in the background. These visors were painted and ornamented with whiskers and beads.

## 22 / *SPREADING THE CANOE*

*Acrylic on canvas.* 16" × 24" (1992). *Collection of Bruce and Linda Colasurdo*

MASTERFULLY DESIGNED CANOES OF MANY SIZES AND FORMS WERE MADE on the Northwest Coast by carving from solid logs. Usually these were of western redcedar, but in some areas Sitka spruce or cottonwood was used. Typically these boats were widened beyond the original diameter of the log by the spreading of the steam-softened sides. Spreading does more than widen the canoe; it introduces major changes of form throughout the hull which the canoe maker must anticipate in carving the log. The straight and level gunwales bend smoothly out and down, while the ends rise, forming a graceful sheer and transforming a rigidly narrow, hollow trough into an elegant watercraft.

In order to spread without splitting, the walls of the hull are made remarkably thin (just over one inch in the 63-foot Northern canoe in the American Museum of Natural History, for example). When the hull is completely carved, water is poured into it (to a depth of 6 inches or so) and is heated to boiling with red-hot rocks. The resulting steam is confined by covering the open hull with mats. The hot rocks are replaced as needed to keep the water at a boil. The softened sides, heated through by the steam inside and fires outside, begin to move outward, aided by the weight of water and rocks pressing down in the center. Spreading sticks are tapped into place between the gunwales and are moved toward the ends and increased in length in the center as the sides flare outward. When the planned beam and form are reached, the canoe is allowed to cool, the water is removed, and the thwarts, bow and stern blocks, and gunwale caps are fitted and fastened in place. Large traveling and war canoes were often painted with designs associated with the names of the canoes or the crests of the owners.

Here, a medium-size Haida canoe is just reaching its finished width; one last load of hot rocks helps to soften the hull thoroughly. As the covering mat is lifted, steam rolls up, partly obscuring the big plank houses with their massive frontal poles on the bank above the beach. Haida canoe makers were widely respected and their products were in demand throughout the northern Northwest Coast. Perhaps this canoe is destined to be taken across Hecate Strait to be traded at the Nass River for eulachon grease, mountain sheep horns, or other mainland products not available on the Queen Charlotte Islands.

## 23 / A CHIEF BY MEANS OF DEEDS

*Acrylic on linen.* 12" × 9" (1993).
*Settlers West Gallery Miniature Show.* Spring 1993

THE PEOPLE OF THE PLAINS TRIBES HONORED MEN WHO EXPOSED
themselves to danger in battle, especially in making hand-to-hand contact with the enemy.
The Crow recognized four major deeds above all others: being the first to touch an enemy;
wresting a gun or bow from an enemy; capturing a horse tethered in an enemy camp; and
successfully leading a war party. A man who had accomplished at least one each of the recognized exploits was called *baatsey'tsey* (good man), a chief because of his deeds. The number
of each man's exploits and their relative merits established the ranking of the chiefs. A man
might have many deeds to his credit, but unless he had accomplished each of the four major
deeds, he was not regarded as a chief.

Two slender sticks wrapped with red and blue trade cloth and tied side-by-side together
form his "long weapon" (*ba-la-xxii-hach-ke*) or coup stick with which to strike the enemy.
The ermine fringe of his beaded war shirt was formerly only allowed to men who had taken
a weapon from an enemy. The heavy, rawhide shield, hung with eagle and hawk feathers and
rimmed with red stroud cloth, is painted with figures from a vision that would bring success
in battle.

## 24 / WAITING OUT THE STORM

*Oil on linen. 14" × 18" (1993). Collection of Bruce and Linda Colasurdo*

ALTHOUGH THE NATIVE PEOPLES OF THE NORTHWEST COAST, AND especially those tribes living along the outer shores of Vancouver Island and the Olympic Peninsula, were expert in the use of canoes in the open sea, there were often times when it was prudent to wait for better weather. An impatient Nuu-chah-nulth paddler, the captain of the large traveling canoe beside him, looks intently out to sea, watching for the sign that the storm will let up so he can assemble his crew and be off. Without his burden of responsibility, the crew are resting in the shelter of the tangled driftwood at the top of the beach. Far to the south, a glimmer of sunlight suggests that the time to pull the big canoe into the diminishing surf may come before long.

The long yew-wood paddle, with its constricted grip and its broad blade with an extended, tapering point, is characteristic of the paddles used by the Westcoast tribes. The black color was produced by smoking the oiled paddle, the blade bound with a protective strip of kelp leaf, over a pitch fire, leaving a decorative band of unsmoked wood crossing the blade. The hat slung on the paddler's back by its chin ties is a distinctive Nuu-chah-nulth style, woven of split spruce root and painted with a black rim and stylized zoomorphic detail in black and red on the crown. His ear pendants are of dentalium shells, fished by these Westcoast people and traded widely to tribes who lacked a source of the prized shell. A white Hudson's Bay Company blanket, pinned over his shoulder, completes his dress. It was the usual overgarment on the coast in the mid-nineteenth century.

## 25 / THE TAUNT

*Oil on linen. 17" × 28" (1993). Collection of Bill and Kathy Brewer*

ON DECEMBER 21, 1866, A COLUMN OF EIGHTY SOLDIERS, HALF INFANTRY
and half cavalry, under the command of Captain William Fetterman, moved out of Fort Phil
Kearney in what is now northern Wyoming to relieve the fort's woodcutters, who were being
attacked by Lakota and Cheyenne warriors. Fort Phil Kearney, more or less constantly ha-
rassed by small war parties, had been established to protect the Bozeman Road, a trail leading
to the Montana goldfields which was a sore point to the Lakota, whose hunting territories it
crossed. On this cold December day, Colonel Henry Carrington, the fort's commanding
officer, worried about Fetterman's impetuousness, had ordered the captain to go directly to
the woodcutters' aid and not to cross the Lodge Trail Ridge. As the column left the fort they
were distracted by a small band of mounted Indians who, milling about just at the limit of
effective firearms range, taunted the troops. One can only wonder why Captain Fetterman,
limited to a fast walk by his infantry, continued to follow the slowly retreating decoys (for that
they were), over the Lodge Trail Ridge in direct violation of his commander's orders, down
to the Bozeman Road, and into a massive ambush of over a thousand Lakota and Cheyenne
warriors who had patiently lain hidden in the freezing December weather. None of Fetterman's command survived.

## 26 / NEZ PERCE SCOUTS AT THE MUSSELSHELL RIVER

*Acrylic on linen.* 14" × 16" (1992). *Collection of Patricia Cosgrove*

IN MID-SEPTEMBER 1877, AFTER ESCAPING THE PURSUING TROOPS AND their Crow allies at the Battle of Canyon Creek near present-day Laurel, Montana, the Nez Perce fugitives moved northward toward their goal of the Canadian border. They were not pursued, so their movement was slowed to allow people and horses to recuperate. Scouts reconnoitered the country in advance, watching for anyone who might prove a danger to the advancing column. These two have reached the Musselshell River near the present town of Ryegate. One wears a blanket capote and is armed with a Springfield carbine and a bow. His companion carries a Winchester '66 in a guncase slung on his back. They have traveled a long, circuitous, and battle-punctuated route since the beginning of their retreat in June, and Canada is only a few days away.

Unfortunately, their goal was not achieved—Colonel Nelson Miles intercepted the Nez Perce at Snake Creek in northern Montana, and a last, bloody battle, ending on October fifth, destroyed their hopes of freedom.

## 27 / THE MOUNTAIN LION SKIN QUIVER

*Acrylic on linen. 16" × 12" (1992). Collection of Wayne and Nancy Badovinus*

A NORTHERN PLAINS WARRIOR OF THE MID—NINETEENTH CENTURY DISPLAYS his brave deeds painted on the buffalo robe he wears. His status as a successful warrior is further attested to by the exploit feathers in his hair, and the hairlocks fringing his pony-beaded leggings. A bowcase-quiver of mountain lion skin, decorated with red trade cloth and pony beads, is slung on his back. These quivers were ingeniously designed, efficiently utilizing the entire lion skin. A strip down the back was sewn into a tube for the quiver, with the attached tail skin hanging from the quiver's mouth. Another strip across the hide, from one front leg to the other, was used for the bowcase, with the two front paws hanging from its ends. Two strips starting at the hind feet and extending up the sides of the skin were sewn together to form the carrying strap. The few scraps left were cut in strips to make the fringes at the base of the quiver and the pendants at the points of attaching the three parts together. The mountain lion skin bowcase-quiver is another interesting example of the common Plains trait of leaving animal skins essentially in their natural shape in the making of clothing and ceremonial regalia.

## 28 / BLUE BEADED GUNCASE

*Acrylic on linen.* 16" × 12" (1993). *Collection of Wayne and Nancy Badovinus*

AN OFFICER OF A BLACKFEET WARRIOR SOCIETY STANDS BESIDE A TRIPOD supporting two fringed, painted rawhide cases, the containers of medicine bundles. The tall, straightup bonnet of quillwork-decorated eagle feathers that he wears is a central object of a similar bundle. It is worn only on ceremonial occasions or in the presence of the enemy. The warrior's dress is of the style of the latter part of the nineteenth century. Heavily beaded guncases with long, trailing fringes, like the one he carries, date from that time. His beaded and fringed shirt retains some of the features of earlier styles, such as the long, hanging hind legs of the antelope skins at the sides. Painted bird tracks and tadpole-like images decorate the upper part of the shirt, which is partially covered with an elaborate beaded "loop necklace," an ornament popular with northern Plains and Plateau men. Red-painted leggings with blue legging strips and wide-cut fringes, solidly beaded, soft-sole moccasins, and a trade cloth breechclout banded with ribbons and brass sequins complete his dress.

Bill Holm © 1993

## 29 / BRASS FINERY

*Acrylic on linen. 16" × 12" (1993). Collection of Wayne and Nancy Badovinus*

MUSLIN SHIRTS WITH NARROW, TORN FRINGES AND SHOULDERS PAINTED red were characteristic of the war dress of a number of northern Plains Indian tribes, but their appearance in Plains warrior pictographs is often an indication of Crow identity. This man is dressed and painted for war. He wears an ermine-covered bonnet with split buffalo horns, feathers, and hanging tubes of ermine skin. A row of brass hawk bells decorates the red stroud browband of the bonnet. Broad bands of ribbed sheet brass encircle his arms, and a war-medicine charm decorated with long-eared owl feathers and an eagle bone whistle hangs on his chest below a brass bead necklace with its pendant disc of conch shell. A pair of long, beaded, and brass-tacked belt pendants hangs over his green stroud breechclout. Brass tacks also decorate the wooden handle of the quirt hanging from the warrior's wrist on a strap of fur and trade cloth. He cradles a Winchester model 1866 carbine, a formidable, rapid-fire weapon. Some of its popularity certainly came from its frame and buttplate of brass, a metal highly prized on the Plains for its decorative qualities.

## 30 / BEAR STRAIGHTUP BONNET

*Acrylic on linen. 16" × 12" (1994). Collection of Paul Raczka*

AMONG THE BLACKFEET OF THE NORTHERN PLAINS, WARBONNETS, especially those with an upright eagle feather crown, were considered powerful war medicine and were treated ceremonially like other medicine bundles. The complex ceremonial handling and care of such a warbonnet bundle ensured its power to make the owner a successful warrior. This bonnet is associated with bear power, demonstrated by the band of bear hide to which the upright feathers are attached. They are wing feathers of young golden eagles, trimmed and dyed red. White ermine pelts and strips of ermine fur cascade from the bear hide foundation, and a long trailer of red trade cloth supports a row of feathers, called "boss ribs" for their resemblance to the upright projections on a buffalo's thoracic vertebrae. "Bear face painting," of red vertical stripes, with black stripes over the eyes and the corners of the mouth, completes the bear power identity of the wearer.

The bonnet wearer dresses elegantly in an ermine-trimmed war shirt, blue trade cloth leggings with beaded panels, and moccasins beaded in a traditional Blackfeet "three-finger" design. Golden eagle tail feathers decorate his yellow-painted coup stick and the rim of his shield, itself the central object of a medicine bundle.

## 31 / FAMILY OUTING

*Acrylic on pressed board. 8" × 15" (1993). Collection of Ellen Ferguson*

ON A STILL SPRING EVENING IN THE EARLY NINETEENTH CENTURY, A COAST Salish family in their traveling canoe (*s.tiwatł*) glide along the southeast coast of Lopez Island. Rolled cattail mats and baskets of provisions are their cargo. Across Rosario Strait, Mount Baker looms in the evening sunlight. The mountain, a dormant volcano, erupted during their lifetime. The Straits Salish name of Mount Baker (*Kulshan*) refers to its volcanic action. Like the other volcanoes in the Cascade Range, it will probably erupt again!

## 32 / EASY MORNING

*Acrylic on canvas.* 9" × 12" (1994). *Collection of Judy Hill*

RESTING ON HIS PADDLE, A HALKOMELEM SALISH MAN DRIFTS IN HIS little *s'naxwit,* an all-purpose canoe of the Juan de Fuca and Georgia straits region. A graceful vessel characterized by a gentle sheer and a deep, angular cutwater, it ranged in length from about two fathoms or armspreads (about twelve feet), to about five fathoms (or thirty feet). This is a small one, very light and handy, drifting lazily on a quiet fall morning. The paddler is in no hurry, enjoying the gentle movement of the canoe. Soon the sun will burn away the lingering fog, and he will be on his way.

## 33 / OH YES! I LOVE YOU, HONEY DEAR

*Acrylic on canvas.* 12" × 9" (1994). *Collection of Marty Holm*

THE SONGS OF THE PLATEAU OWL DANCE ARE LOVE SONGS AND OFTEN incorporate English phrases, like that in the title of the painting. Here two young singers at the turn of the century, members of the Yakama tribe, accompany their song on hand drums. The singers for the Owl and Rabbit Dances, which are danced in couples, or the Circle Dances, which usually alternate men and women, traditionally stand in the center of the dance floor, accompanying their singing with single-headed hand drums. This differs from the War Dance, the popular men's social dance, in which the singers all sit around a big drum at one end of the dance house.

The singers wear panel leggings of the Plateau type, and the long loop necklaces that were characteristic of Plateau and northern Plains festival dress. Their beaded belt pouches and tack-studded panel belts with long, decorated pendants were essential elements of men's fancy dress. One singer carries a coyote skin war medicine and wears otter skin braid wraps. The long, plaid shawl breechclout was another common feature of men's dress at the time.

## 34 / MEXICANA AND SUTIL
## IN GUEMES CHANNEL, JUNE 11, 1792

*Acrylic on linen.* 18" × 28" (1995). *Collection of James Richardson*

NEAR MIDDAY OF JUNE 11, 1792, TWO SMALL SPANISH SHIPS, *SUTIL* AND *Mexicana*, under the commands of the young Frigate Captains Don Dionisio Alcalá-Galiano and Don Cayetano Valdés y Flores, sailed into Guemes Channel near the present city of Anacortes, Washington. Their mission was to explore and chart the waterways inside Juan de Fuca Strait and to attempt to locate the fabled "Northwest Passage" to the Atlantic. The two little ships (about 45 feet on the waterline) had sailed here from Acapulco in southern Mexico via Nootka Sound, where they had been refitted and provisioned. The evening before, they had anchored off the southeast point of Lopez Island and a party had gone ashore to observe the emergence of the first moon of Jupiter in order to correct their longitude. This observation was probably made on what is today part of my property on Watmough Head, Lopez Island!

The light, following breeze was not strong enough to allow the two ships to buck the tidal current in the center of Guemes Channel, so they closed the south shore to take advantage of the side eddies along Fidalgo Island. Four young Indians and an older man from the village on Guemes Island paddled expertly out to the ships and traded blackberries, dried clams, and a dog-wool robe lined with feathers, for buttons and beads. The young artist on *Mexicana*, José Cardero, captured the incident in a spectacular painting now in the Museo Naval in Madrid. His view of the two ships in Guemes Channel, with Mount Baker looming on the horizon, was the inspiration for this painting of a setting very familiar to me.

I am much indebted to Mark Myers, RSMA, F/ASMA, for detailed information on the two ships, and especially for his interpretation of José Cardero's drawings of the unusual rigging of *Mexicana*'s main mast.

## 35 / FIRST SAIL

*Acrylic on linen.* 18" × 24" (1995). *Collection of Nancy Davenport*

A MOWACHAHT SEAL HUNTER IS SURPRISED TO SEE ON THE HORIZON THE first European ship to approach Vancouver Island. The Spanish frigate *Santiago*, Captain Juan Pérez, was returning to Mexico from a voyage to Alaska, undertaken primarily to ascertain the extent of the Russian presence on the Northwest Coast. On the way north, Pérez had met and traded with Haida Indians at the northwestern tip of the Queen Charlotte Islands, apparently the first contact that those people had with Europeans. A few objects now in the Museo de America in Madrid (among them a beautiful ivory bird amulet) form the earliest collection known from the Northwest Coast.

On August 8, 1774, on the way south, the *Santiago* approached the west coast of Vancouver Island and anchored in the vicinity of the entrance to Nootka Sound. Mowachaht canoes gathered around the ship, and again the Spanish seamen traded for artifacts from the Indians. A boat sent shoreward with a wooden cross, intended to mark the spot where the ceremony of possession was to take place, was forced to return to the ship when the weather changed for the worse. This fleeting contact was the basis on which the Spanish claimed sovereignty in the area, and it was the first meeting of Nuu-chah-nulth (Nootkan) people with white men, whose ships, following Captain James Cook's anchorage in Nootka Sound four years later, came in increasing numbers until the end of the sea otter trade.

The hunter holds his long seal harpoon, ready to make the cast. Its double prongs are armed with barbed points that detach from the harpoon on striking the quarry. A line of braided sea lion gut runs from the points, through a retaining loop on the shaft, to a float made of an inflated seal stomach or to a thwart of the canoe. When the seal is brought to the canoe, the hunter kills it with a wooden club, here propped in the bow. His robe of shredded yellowcedar bark, twined with nettle-fiber cord, is belted at the waist. To free his arms for the cast, the robe's upper part, with its sea otter fur–wrapped headline, is folded down. It was this fur that drew the flotillas of trading ships to the Northwest Coast in the waning years of the century.

## 36 / YAKAMA SUNSET

*Acrylic on linen.* 35" × 26" (1995). *Collection of Natalie Fay Linn*

THE GALA DRESS AND ELABORATE HORSE GEAR OF A YOUNG YAKAMA woman reflect the warm color of the setting sun. The yoke of her trade cloth dress is covered with rows of dentalium shells from the coast which were highly prized by the Plateau people. Fur trading companies early recognized their value and imported thousands of the shells, obtained in trade from the tribes along the west coast of Vancouver Island. The richly beaded belt, blanket strip, and saddle are the transmontane style, shared by the Crow people of Montana, but her double saddle-bag with its long fringes, the flat bag hung on the prong of the saddle pommel, and the broad horsecollar, all made of twined textile decorated with corn-husk false embroidery, are distinctive of the tribes of the Columbia Plateau. Both the saddle-bag and the horsecollar are made of recycled flat bags, cut apart and reassembled in new form. Brass bells add to their effect. Unique to the Plateau is the twined, tapered woman's hat, with its complex pattern of elaborated triangles. Her necklaces of shell disc beads, called "wampum" on the Plateau, and faceted cylindrical beads of cobalt blue glass, called "Hudson's Bay beads" or "Russian beads," are typical Plateau finery. Long strips of otter fur wrap the young woman's braids, topped with earrings of broad conch shell discs that echo the nearly full moon rising behind her.

## 37 / THE STRIKE

*Acrylic on linen.* 18" × 24" (1995). *Collection of the Canadian Museum of Civilization*

HUMPBACK AND GRAY WHALES, MIGRATING ALONG THE OUTER COASTS OF Vancouver Island and Washington State's Olympic Peninsula, were the most prestigious prey of Nuu-chah-nulth and Makah sea hunters, who pursued the whales in cedar canoes in the open Pacific. Whales that were successfully killed and towed back to the whalers' village, as well as dead whales that drifted to shore, were important sources of meat, oil, bone, and sinew. But the economic importance of whaling was far overshadowed by its prestige. Harpooning a whale was an inherited chiefly privilege, and a successful whaler was honored far beyond his own time. Ritual preparation for the hunt was long and arduous, and the loss of a whale was usually attributed to some failure on the part of a crewman to follow carefully all the ceremonial requirements. Even with all care, effort, and skill, the success rate was not high. John Jewitt, describing the Mowachaht chief Maqquina's whaling in 1803, 1804, and 1805, counted fifty-three days of hunting in which one whale was killed and several were lost.

The canoe used in whaling was fairly beamy for its length of about six fathoms (or outstretched arms) in order to accommodate its crew of eight—the harpooner, six paddlers, a steersman—and the whaling gear itself: the heavy yew-wood harpoon shaft, up to fourteen feet long, the mussel shell–bladed point and its whale sinew lanyard, up to one hundred fathoms of cedar withe line, four inflated floats of hair seal skin, a killing lance, and spare shaft, points and uninflated floats. All of this combined to make a bulky load. Provisions and water were needed, especially if a harpooned whale ran seaward and required a long tow home.

The whaling canoe approached the whale's left side, and at the proper moment, just before the whale dived, the harpooner struck it behind the flipper. As the harpoon struck, the paddlers in turn cast the floats and line overboard and turned the canoe away from the struggling whale. With luck and proper ritual preparation, the whale ran toward land. When it had tired enough, the whalers approached again and killed the whale with a lance. Then began the long paddle back to the beach and the butchering. A cut of skin and blubber including the dorsal fin was ceremonially prepared and displayed in the whaler's house, to honor both the whale and its captor.

*The Strike* depicts the moment before the whaler casts his harpoon. His quarry, a humpback whale, is about to dive, after having surfaced several times to breathe. The canoe is of an early style, with long, forward-thrust prow, less upright than later models. A Lightning Serpent, the harpoon of the Thunderbird, is painted on the hull. The first paddler is preparing to cast overboard his seal skin float, with its red and black ownership designs.

## 38 / THE COUP COUNTER

*Acrylic on canvas.* 12" × 9" (1996). *Collection of Gary Spratt*

A SUCCESSFUL CROW WAR PARTY LEADER RECREATES AN ENCOUNTER WITH
the enemy before an audience of his peers. His standing as a warrior depended upon the
number and personal danger of his exploits, and ideally the deeds should have been witnessed and corroborated by his comrades in battle. Painted and dressed as for war, he carries
a decorated pipe-tomahawk and his vision-inspired shield, a powerful war medicine. It is
hung with a summer weasel skin and the tail feathers of marsh harriers, Cooper's hawks,
immature redtail hawks, and red-shafted flickers. The whole, stuffed skin of another flicker
is tied in his hair, following the instructions of his vision. His black-painted buckskin shirt,
fringed with hair-locks, is an emblem of a successful war party leader.

## 39 / THE BUFFALO RUNNER

*Acrylic on linen (mounted on pressed board). 7" × 14" (1996).*

THE INTRODUCTION OF THE HORSE OPENED THE GREAT PLAINS AREA TO widespread occupation and easier utilization of its vast resources, especially the enormous herds of buffalo. The preferred technique of tribal hunts changed from the ancient buffalo jump (stampeding the herds over selected cliffs) to one of riding into the herds and killing individual animals with arrows, or "buffalo running." Horses that were fast, agile, and bold enough to run in the milling herd were selected and trained especially for the task. Known as "buffalo runners," these horses were highly prized by their owners. They were usually picketed next to the tipi to protect them from marauding enemies, for whom they were a special prize. In the hunt, the buffalo runners were typically led by the hunters when approaching the herd and were mounted only when the chase began.

A Crow hunter leads his buffalo runner on the way to the village hunt. This one is also favored for his gaudy coat, made even fancier by the eagle feathers tied in his tail.

## 40 / A GOOD TRADE

*Acrylic on linen. 24" × 36" (1997). Collection of Georg and Christa Barth*

IN THE NINETEENTH CENTURY THE NEZ PERCE OF THE EASTERN COLUMBIA River Plateau and the Mountain Crow of the Yellowstone River area enjoyed a mutually beneficial relationship that included the sharing of hunting grounds, the trading of goods and materials that were unavailable to the trading partners, and the bonding of marriage between the two tribes. A style of beaded art that has been called "transmontane" developed along with this relationship, most clearly seen in Crow beadwork of the latter half of the nineteenth century. The closeness of this intertribal friendship diminished when, in the 1877 "Nez Perce War," expected help from the Crows failed to materialize.

When the Nez Perce traveled to "the buffalo country" for hunting and visiting, they brought with them, among goods of their country, fine horses and woven bags filled with dried roots. Finely tanned buffalo robes were among the trade goods they took in exchange. Here in a Crow camp in Montana, a Nez Perce woman and her Crow trading partner complete such an exchange. Everyone is in festival dress, and the Plateau woman is wearing her fine dress of mountain sheep skins, heavily decorated with lanes of pony beads, and her hat woven of Indian hemp and grass. She carries her baby in a cradle board suspended from a carrying strap across her shoulders. The Crow woman wears a trade cloth dress decorated with elk teeth, or bone replicas. The dress is in the early "wing dress" style, rather than the later, sleeved pattern of Crow wear. Her beaded moccasins, belt, and knife sheath illustrate the transmontane style, fully developed by the 1870s.

A Crow girl entertains her Nez Perce playmate with her doll in a typical Crow cradle, while their brothers play at war! A group of men admire a fine Appaloosa horse brought across the mountains by the Nez Perce. His rider wears an antelope hide shirt decorated with bands of porcupine quill–wrapped horsehair, a style worn by both Plateau and Crow men. A Crow chief wears his ermine-fringed beaded shirt and trade cloth leggings and carries an elaborate "mirror bag." His tribesmate is wrapped in a robe of red and green trade cloth with a broad, beaded blanket strip, common to both sides of the mountains.

Crow/Nez Perce gatherings often led to romance, and marriage between the two groups was not uncommon. Two couples shown here riding among the tipis suggest that these relationships will continue!

## 41 / THE LAST CHANCE

*Acrylic on linen.* 18" × 24" (1997). *Collection of Donn Charnley*

ON A STILL, MOONLIT NIGHT IN THE CLOSING YEARS OF THE NINETEENTH century a group of Kwakwaka'wakw Indians, pausing on their trip home from the hop fields in the Puget Sound country, gamble on a beach in the San Juan Islands. Their big fifty-foot traveling canoes are drawn up on the beach for the night. They are playing *lehal* or *s'lahal* (*alaxwa* in their language), the bone game, one of the most widespread and still popular gambling games of Native North America. Accompanied by rousing songs and the percussion of sticks and drums, the game becomes almost a dance, as the bone handlers gesture and sway to the driving rhythm and the "pointer" and his associates on the guessing team try to confuse them with feints and false guesses. The pointer's object is to choose the location of the unmarked two (of the four) bone cylinders concealed in the hands of his opponents. His choice of the four possible locations—both right, both left, both inside, both outside—is indicated by hand signals, making play possible across linguistic boundaries. The many tribes gathered at the hop fields met often in *lehal*, where their exhilarant songs could be heard throughout the nights. This one is a friendly game, but stakes are always required, and blankets and money from hop-picking wages (wrapped in a scarf) are piled on the beach between the teams.

The ten counting sticks have shifted from team to team as the game has progressed. Now, however, the pointer's side has only two left, and the outcome depends on his skill and gambling power to reverse the flow. He and his teammates concentrate their powers on the bone handlers, and he studies their eyes and gestures for any indication of the location of the white bones. With a combination of luck, skill, and supernatural power, he makes his decision. Out goes the signal, outspread thumb and fingers, with a decisive slap of hand on arm, to indicate "both outside." His last chance has gone, as the bone holders triumphantly throw open their hands to show the unmarked bones "inside!" The game is over. The victors gather up their winnings, and all retire for the night, to resume their leisurely 200-mile paddle home (with perhaps more *lehal*) in the morning.

## 42 / THE HIGH RIDGE

*Acrylic on linen. 24" × 18" (1997). Collection of John Putnam*

A SHOSHONE HORSEMAN, SCOUTING AHEAD OF HIS MOVING VILLAGE, PAUSES on the summit of a high ridge to scout the sweeping country ahead for signs of activity. The movements of buffalo or other animals indicate to him the presence or absence of humans, many of whom are potential enemies. It is the mid-nineteenth century, and tribal enmities are still strong.

The scout is armed with a bow and lance, tipped with an iron trade blade. He is an experienced and successful warrior, judging by the scalp decorating the lance, the coup feather in his hair, and his grizzly claw necklace. Trade materials—his muslin shirt and brass armbands, the cloth, beads, and brass buttons on his quirt strap, and the blanket capote draping his pony's withers—indicate the long Shoshone contact with American traders.

## 43 / SUN PAINTS HIS CHEEKS

*Acrylic on linen. 6" × 29" (1997). Collection of Lloyd J. Averill*

WHEN THE SUN, LYING NEAR THE HORIZON, IS SWEPT ACROSS ITS FACE BY wispy *cirrus* clouds laden with ice crystals, "sun dogs" may appear. Glowing spots of light flank and mimic the sun, giving to the phenomenon its scientific name of *parhelia*, or "mock suns." While not uncommon, it is often overlooked, except in the northern latitudes, where it can be bright and colorful enough to be very impressive to all who see it.

Sun Dogs appear in the mythology and lore of many northern tribes and have been called by many descriptive names—*Sun Paints his Cheeks* by the Blackfeet, *Sun Kindles a Fire* by the Lakota, and *The Abalone Shell Earrings of the Sun* by the Kwakwa̱ka'wakw, for example. Particularly bright, multiple, or unusually shaped appearances were often considered omens, such as might predict the death of a chief.

On a winter hilltop in northern Montana, a group of Blackfeet horsemen gather to observe the "Sun painting his cheeks."

## 44 / SUN, MOON, AND STAR

*Acrylic, cotton seine twine, epoxy filler, on canvas-covered hardboard.* 10" × 12" (1997).

*Collection of Edward Marcuse*

"SUN, MOON, AND STAR" (*TL!ISALABALIS, MAKWALABALIS, T!OT!OBALIS*) is one of the vast array of figures known to Kwakwaka'wakw people which are made by manipulating a loop of string with the fingers. Techniques of producing string-figures are known to peoples around the world, and some North American cultures, Eskimo and Navajo for example, have prodigious repertoires. Kwakwaka'wakw examples range from simple, one-movement examples, like the "Jumping Sand-flea," to complex narrative illustrations, often accompanied by dialog or song, where a younger brother jumps past his older brother, an old woman crosses a river, a canoe capsizes and throws its crew into the water, salmon jump from stream after stream in Knight Inlet, and on and on. Some are illustrations of myths, and some are competitive, designed to best other string-figure makers.

The late Kwakwaka'wakw chief Mungo Martin and his wife Abayah were experts, and my wife Marty and I spent many an evening, long into the night, trying to emulate their graceful, rhythmic movements in bringing the string loop to life. One of the first complex figures we learned was "Sun, Moon, and Star." Abayah was particularly adept, and I have tried to show her here, forming the interlocking loops of that figure. Behind her appear two old photographs. One, by Edward Curtis, is of the young *Tl!akwagilayugwa* (Abayah's noble name) in the dress of the Weather Dancer. The other shows her family, with her, at about two years of age, holding her father's great copper.

## 45 / WELCOME DANCE

*Acrylic on linen.* 14" × 18" (1997). *Collection of Kodi Nelson*

AS CANOES BEARING GUESTS INVITED TO A POTLATCH AT 'YALIS SLOWLY
approach the shore, they are greeted by a Welcome Dance. White eagle down scattered
from the crown of the dancer's headdress swirls around him as a symbol of peace and solemn
ceremony. The richness of his dress—carved headdress with its ermine trailer, copper-design
button blanket, and elaborate raven rattle—honors the rank of the arriving chiefs. The host
stands ready to greet the guests and invite them ashore for his hospitality—"The fire is ready."
The double-headed serpent Sisiutl, grasped by a Thunderbird, forms his headdress and is
repeated in the figures on his talking stick.

The time is the 1890s, but with the revival of canoe-making in the 1990s, it could just
as well be a century later. The dress and regalia of the participants has hardly changed today,
and the view from Alert Bay across Broughton Strait to Vancouver Island is very much as it
was in those earlier days.

The picture was painted for an auction to benefit the rebuilding of the ceremonial
big-house at Alert Bay, which had been destroyed in an arson fire. Just a year and a half later,
in May 1999, a flotilla of newly made canoes brought chiefs of the Kwakwaka'wakw villages
and other tribes to the beach at 'Yalis, just as in the painting, for the great celebration of the
dedication of the new big-house.

## 46 / HIDATSA BLACKMOUTH WARRIOR

*Acrylic on linen.* 12" × 9" (1998). *Collection of Gary Spratt*

THE BLACKMOUTH SOCIETY (*EE'ICHIPEE'A*) WAS ONE OF A SERIES OF warrior associations shared by the Hidatsa and their neighbors, the Mandan, earth-lodge dwellers along the Missouri River in present-day North Dakota. The members of the Blackmouth Society were generally seasoned warriors. Since they were the principal enforcers of village law, they were also called "The Soldiers." Among their emblems was a curved warclub with a knife blade inserted at the bend, here seen as a "gunstock" club with a trade "stabber" blade. The mid-nineteenth-century warrior wears a headdress crowned with narrow, "split" buffalo horns mounted on a cap covered with strips of ermine. Eagle tail feathers, some dyed red, stream as a trailer down his back. His shirt and robe are decorated with bands of porcupine quill embroidery, a style of decoration favored by the Hidatsa, and continued by Hidatsa quillworkers into this century. The shirt strips and the panels of his blanket strip are made with the multiple-quill plaiting technique, while the rosettes are in quill-wrapped horsehair, all bordered with single lanes of pony-beadwork. Partially quill-wrapped thongs pendant from the rosettes are embellished with beaver claws.

## 47 / BIRD SKIN TUNIC

*Acrylic on linen.* 18" × 24" (1998). *Collection of David and Betty Stephens*

TO FORM DRESS TUNICS, KODIAK ISLAND WOMEN SEWED TOGETHER THE iridescent-feathered neck skins of pelagic cormorants, ornamenting them with bands of fine skin and hair embroidery, accented with ermine fur. On this tunic, pairs of red-dyed strips of sea lion esophagus membrane, also tufted with ermine, fringe the decorated bands. This is festive clothing, and the hunter here is dressed for display rather than for making practical use of his elegant bird spear and *atlatl*, or throwing stick. The Kodiak carvers produced among the most beautiful of atlatls, the conventional design said to be an abstract image of a sea otter.

Living in a transitional zone between the Northwest Coast Tlingits and the Bering Sea Eskimo, the people of Kodiak utilized forms and techniques from both areas, most clearly seen here in the twined spruce-root hat of the hunter. Very much like Tlingit hats in form, and painted in a unique Pacific Eskimo variant of Tlingit design, hats of this region were often profusely decorated with beads, dentalium shells, and sea lion whiskers, symbolizing the wearer's prowess as a hunter.

Pelagic cormorants, the source of the skins used in this tunic, swim beyond the hunter, or streak over the North Pacific waters. It is said that to make one tunic requires the neck skins of one hundred fifty birds.

The 18th- and early 19th-century Russian occupants of southwestern Alaska called the Kodiak Islands *Aleut* or *Koniag*. Today the people prefer to be called *Alutiiq* or *Sugpiaq* (a Real Person).

## 48 / THE SPANISH BROAD SWORD

*Acrylic on linen.* 27" × 18" (1998).
*De Facto* magazine. Brussels. 1999 (20).

THE EARLY DECADES OF THE NINETEENTH CENTURY WERE A PERIOD OF elaboration in the festival dress of the people of the Plains. The Crow and their Hidatsa kinsmen were especially known for the elegance of their appearance. Men who were successful in war displayed their accomplishments by means of military insignia and a record of their exploits painted on their clothing. Here, a brave man wears a shirt and leggings and carries a buffalo robe, all emblazoned with pictographic evidence of deeds, recording his capture of weapons, defeat of enemies, leadership, and generosity. He carries an antique Spanish cavalry broad sword from the colonies in the Southwest, which, like the horse and its gear, has made its way through warfare or intertribal trade to the upper Missouri country. That it is an honorable weapon is shown by the fan of eagle feathers hung from the pommel and the four painted representations of the sword on his shirt, one of which can be seen just above the quilled blanket strip.

The paintings on the shirt, leggings, and robe of this proud warrior are examples of the work of a single, unknown artist whose distinctive style of pictography sets him apart from his contemporaries. The shirt and leggings he wears are from the collection in the Opočno Castle in the Czech Republic, and his buffalo robe is in the National Museum of Denmark. All three are embellished with bands of quillwork, in multi-quill plaiting and in single and double bundle quill-wrapped horsehair, bordered with beads.

## 49 / HOYLIK̲ALAⱢ

*Acrylic on canvas.* 30" × 22" (1999).

*Indian Summer Exhibition, Royal Museums of Art and History.* Brussels, Belgium. 1999

*Indian Summer: Les Premiers Nations de l'Amerique du Nord.* Brussels, Belgium. 1999

THE HOYLIK̲ALAⱢ (WHICH CAN BE TRANSLATED "HEALING DANCER") IS THE highest ranking dancer of the Kwakwa̲ka'wakw ceremonial complex, Tⱡa'sa̲la. The ceremony is sometimes called the Feather Dance (after the eagle down that is scattered by the headdress), Weasel Dance (after the ermine skins that embellish it), or Peace Dance, a name common to all the tribes that use the elaborate headdress. The Tⱡa'sa̲la ceremony came to the Kwakwa̲ka'wakw in marriage from the North, along with the headdress and the Raven rattle.

The Hoylika̲laⱡ wears dramatic regalia. A family history, recorded by George Hunt, of the acquisition of the Tⱡa'sa̲la ceremony by marriage from the Bella Bella, describes the dancer shaking a raven rattle and wearing a black bear skin robe, a cedar bark neckring, and a dancing headdress with ermine skins. In historic times his robe has typically been a blanket bordered with red cloth and ornamented with patterns worked in pearl buttons, although dancers with Tlingit ancestry may wear an inherited Chilkat blanket. A wooden plaque, elaborately carved with a crest figure and inlaid with abalone shell, is attached to the forehead of the headdress, and a long trailer shingled with white ermine skins falls over the dancer's back. Long whiskers of the northern sea lion rise from the top and enclose a loose mass of white eagle down that is scattered from the headdress with the dancer's movements, drifting through the firelight around him.

As his first song begins, accompanied by a fast, rolling beat, the Hoylika̲laⱡ emerges from behind a painted screen at the back of the house. He dances low, nearly kneeling, with arms outstretched, spreading his glittering robe. At each change of rhythm, he turns with several steps, head bowed, and takes up his crouching stance in another direction. When his second song begins, he stands and dances, turning and nodding to spread the floating down with quick tosses of his headdress. An attendant, called Dⱡakwemiⱡ ("standing alongside in the house"), shaking a copper-shaped rattle, watches the dancer. A similar copper is held by the Dzunuk̲'wa carved on the housepost looming beside him.

# Chronology & Bibliography

## LLOYD J. AVERILL

I T WAS THE SUMMER OF 1934. NINE-YEAR-OLD BILL HOLM WAS looking for something to fill the spare hours on a family visit to Grandmother and Grandfather Gerntholz, who lived with two adult sons and a daughter at their farm home in North Dakota. A devoted reader at any time, Bill found his way into the room that housed Uncle Albert's library and, browsing, came upon an arresting title: *Two Little Savages, Being the Adventures of Two Boys Who Lived as Indians and What They Learned. With Over Three Hundred Drawings.*

Taking the book from the shelf, he read the first sentence: "Yan was much like other twelve-year-old boys in having a keen interest in Indians and in wild life. . . ." In fact, Yan was much like Bill himself, who had been photographed in a store-bought "Indian" tunic and headdress two days after his fourth birthday, and whose interest in wildlife had been nurtured early under the big sky of his small-town, south-central Montana home.

Hooked—identified—by that first sentence, the nine-year-old read on to the end of the 550-page book, absorbed by the adventures of Yan and Sam, the two Canadian white boys of Ernest Thompson Seton's title. He visualized himself imitating what Yan and Sam imagined Indian life to be—raising tipis, making bows and arrows, drums, and other artifacts, stalking and hunting animals, learning to live on the land—and he was eager to get on with that imitation. In fact, before leaving the North Dakota farm, Bill went out into a nearby grove of trees and made a tipi out of sticks and blankets. Seeing his nephew's enthusiasm, Uncle Albert made him a present of the book—he still has it — and it became the initial traveler's guide to a world of increasingly serious preoccupation through all of his subsequent years.

Indeed, to this outside observer there seems to be something remarkably prescient in the opening words of Seton's book. Bill Holm, while acknowledging a direct continuity from that 1934 moment into the active present, is too sober an interpreter to put it that way. Here, so that the reader may judge, is a full account of its opening paragraph:

Yan was much like other twelve-year-old boys in having a keen interest in Indians and in wild life, but he differed from most in this, that he never got over it. Indeed, as he grew older, he found a yet keener pleasure in storing up the little bits of woodcraft and Indian lore that pleased him as a boy. [New York: Grosset & Dunlap, 1903, p. 19]

And where has that 1934 moment led? To the distinguished career, as artist and art historian, of a man from Roundup, Montana, who, at an early age, was captivated by the Native American culture and "never got over it."

## CHRONOLOGY

1925      Oscar William Holm, Jr., and his twin sister Elizabeth were born on March 24 in Roundup, Montana, to Martha and Oscar Holm. With the exception of military and university records, he has been "Bill" throughout his life. Oscar Holm, Sr., was an electrician; Martha Holm was a teacher in the public schools.

1925–37      Bill engaged in drawing and crafts from early childhood, inspired by the Native culture of Montana, and by his reading, at age nine, of *Two Little Savages*, by Ernest Thompson Seton.

1937      The family moved to Seattle, seeking to escape the Montana summers that exacerbated Bill's asthma. They bought a house in the Woodland Park–Green Lake neighborhood for easy access for Bill and sister Betty, by bicycle or bus, to the University of Washington campus. Martha Holm took Bill for his first visit to the Washington State Museum (now the Burke Museum of Natural History and Culture), where Bill began his enduring friendship with Dr. Erna Gunther, the museum's director. Dr. Gunther introduced young Bill to her Makah friends in Neah Bay and took him to Spirit Dances in the Swinomish smokehouse near LaConner, thus initiating his direct contact with Native people, their ceremonies, and their art. Bill found the Spirit Dances especially compelling.

1937–43    As a ninth-grader, in what Bill characterizes as his "first professional act as a
           Northwest Coast scholar," he served as "technical adviser" to a seventh-grade
           art class production of a Northwest Coast–based play, *Tuteka and the Bear*. He
           sketched ideas and made drawings based on objects from the museum, and he
           arranged through Dr. Gunther to borrow masks and a canoe for the production.

           His interest in Plains and Plateau culture continued through his friendship
           with Roger Ernesti, a graduate student in anthropology and a museum staffer, and
           with Ernesti's Yakama friends, who invited him to visit the Yakama reservation to
           observe the dances.

           At Lincoln High School, he organized a small group that performed Plains
           and Plateau dances in the community, using some authentic regalia as well as
           pieces made by members of the group.

1940–41    In the summers, Bill worked at the Cub Scout Camp Edmond Meany as Indian
           Lore Counselor and bugler.

1942       Bill began what was to be a 54-year association with the Henderson Camps (later
           Camp Nor'wester) in Washington's San Juan Islands. He joined the counseling
           staff for the summer of 1942, and again in 1943, prior to his entering military
           service.

1943–45    After graduating from Lincoln High School, Bill was ordered to report for induc-
           tion into the United States Army. He completed infantry training at Camp Fan-
           nin, Texas, and was sent to an Army Specialized Training Program in engineering
           at Pomona College in southern California. Because of the need for ground troops
           in Europe, however, the program closed in three months. After being briefly as-
           signed to a tank battalion, he trained with a newly formed Field Artillery Obser-
           vation battalion and was posted to the front lines in France, where his earlier
           experience and training in drawing served him well in the panoramic sketching
           of artillery targets.

           With the end of the war in Europe, Bill was sent back to the States. When
           the Pacific war ended, he was mustered out at Ft. Lewis, Washington, as a master
           sergeant.

1946       In January, he enrolled as an undergraduate in the University of Washington
           School of Art, to major in painting. That spring, he helped to prepare the newly
           relocated Henderson Camps on Lopez Island for the 1946 season. Until 1966
           (with the exception of 1950), Bill taught Native arts at the camp every summer.

He re-established his friendship with Roger Ernesti, dancing with him at pow-wows in eastern Washington. Ernesti's Yakama friends arranged a "giveaway" in Bill's honor, at which he was initiated into the Toppenish Longhouse and given the Yakama name *Shiakla* (Scout, or Sees the enemy), in recognition of his wartime experience as an artillery spotter. He also joined a small group of Seattle friends, self-styled "The Ikpoos," to perform Plains, Plateau, and Northwest Coast dancing throughout the Puget Sound area. With a group of students presenting programs of American folk dances, he toured Sweden during the summer of 1950.

1949     After graduating from the University of Washington (elected to Phi Beta Kappa; awarded the Bachelor of Fine Arts degree, *magna cum laude*), Bill immediately entered the Master of Fine Arts program at the UW, again in painting.

1951     He received the Master of Fine Arts degree. Thesis: "The Northwest Coast—Sea, Mountains, Forest, Dance," a series of four oil paintings done in a semi-abstract style.

1953     In August, Bill married Martha (Marty) Mueller, whom he had met in 1949 on the staff of the Henderson Camps. In the fall, he joined the art faculty of Lincoln High School in Seattle, where he had graduated ten years earlier.

      As a guest of curator Wilson Duff of the British Columbia Provincial Museum, Bill attended the first potlatch to be celebrated since the removal (in 1951) of the anti-potlatch laws from Canada's Indian Act. The potlatch was given by Kwakiutl Chief Mungo Martin, the museum's master carver, in a new big-house at the museum, built under Martin's direction. This was Bill's first direct exposure to authentic Kwakwa̱ka'wakw ceremony.

1955     After visiting Kwakwa̱ka'wakw villages by kayak with Marty, Bill directed the erection of a big-house at Camp Nor'wester on Lopez Island. In subsequent years, he carved a number of free-standing poles scattered about the campgrounds, and he painted flat designs on the walls and doors of camp buildings.

1957     Bill invited Mungo Martin and his family to attend an August "play potlatch" at the new big-house on Lopez Island. When they arrived, Mungo's granddaughter, Helen Hunt, said of her grandfather: "He can't believe his eyes, that what he sees here is actually happening, just like in olden times!" Mungo Martin was lead singer that night, and he gave eloquent speeches in the Kwakwala language. He gave Bill one of his grandfather's names—*Na̱msga̱muti* (He speaks only once)—and his wife, Abayah, gave to Marty Holm the name *Na̱x̱wit̓* (Light in the house).

      Many Native artists came to the play potlatches in subsequent years, including Haida artist Bill Reid. Reid said that his enthusiasm for Kwakiutl art had been enhanced by seeing, on two occasions, "masks and costumes displayed as they should be . . . in sensitively conceived re-enactments by Bill Holm and his dancers." Mungo and Abayah Martin returned many times, until Mungo Martin's death in 1962.

1958 Bill received his Standard General Teaching Certificate. While completing certification requirements, he wrote a research paper for Erna Gunther laying out his informal observations of the structure of northern Coastal art. This led to further systematic research which culminated in his groundbreaking book, *Northwest Coast Indian Art: An Analysis of Form* (1965), presenting the theoretical foundation for the new discipline of Northwest Coast Native art history. Still in print, the book is today considered a classic.

He carved his first canoe, a 24-foot Kwakwaka'wakw-style craft, on the beach at Camp Nor'wester.

1959 At a potlatch on Turnour Island, Mungo Martin brought Bill out as a Hamat´sa dancer, with a name Martin had previously given him: *Hamtsi'stesalagalis* (Unrestrained Hamat´sa everywhere). Bill was sometimes referred to by other Kwakwaka'wakw as "Mungo's Hamat´sa," and a song composed for Bill says: "I am the only Hamat´sa beyond the edge of the world" (i.e., across the international boundary). At this time Martin gave Bill the name *Ho'miskanis* (Plenty of everything), the name by which he is known at Kwakwaka'wakw potlatches. Abayah Martin gave Marty Holm one of her own Winter Dance names: *Heligaxstegalis* (Taming the Hamat´sa everywhere); and Mungo Martin gave her the name *Dladlawikagilakw* (Ready to stand up for her family in potlatching). Later, names and dance privileges were also given to daughters Carla and Karen Holm.

1953–68 At various times over his fifteen years at Lincoln, Bill taught painting, drawing, sculpture, and printmaking. As a fill-in for absent teachers, he also taught lettering and changed a course in fashion design to fashion illustration. He painted large sets for school dramatic productions, designed covers for student publications and screen-prints for student activities, and organized student art fairs.

1960 Daughter Carla was born on February 15. She was given the name *Tsekefilakw* (Ready to give the Winter Ceremonial) by Mungo Martin.

1961 Bill was invited to teach at Port Chilkoot, near Haines, Alaska, at a school established to teach indigenous arts to Tlingits from nearby communities. He taught in the school periodically until 1966.

1962 Daughter Karen was born on March 12.

In September and October, Bill visited museums in the U.S. and Canada, photographing over 200 masks used in the Kwakwaka'wakw Hamat'sa ceremony. Then, in November and December, from a base in Alert Bay, B.C., with his family he carried the photographs to nearby villages, asking dancers, carvers, and chiefs what they knew about the masks and noting their comments. It was his most intensive contact to date with Kwakwaka'wakw country.

On a visit to curator George Irving Quimby at Chicago's Field Museum of Natural History, Bill learned of the existence of a copy of Edward Curtis's 1914 film *In the Land of the Head-Hunters*, and he became determined to find a way to show the film to Kwakwaka'wakw elders for their interpretation of its contents.

1964      Daughter Karen received the War Dance privilege and the name *Sabalkeł* (Copper sound in the house) from Mrs. Peter Smith.

1966      Bill received the Washington State Governor's Writer's Award for *Northwest Coast Indian Art: An Analysis of Form* (Seattle: University of Washington Press, 1965).

1967      For the library at Lincoln High School, he painted a 5′ × 30′ mural of Captain George Vancouver's ship, *Discovery*, anchored off Restoration Point (on what is now Bainbridge Island in Puget Sound), surrounded by Indian canoes.

With a 16mm copy of the 1914 Curtis film *In the Land of the Head-Hunters*, Bill traveled with Marty and daughters Carla and Karen to several Kwakwaka'wakw villages, showing the film to people who had participated in or had been present at the filming fifty-three years earlier, recording their comments. He decided that a soundtrack, using the voices and songs of some of these people, could be made for the film.

1968      He carved his 35-foot Haida-style canoe on the beach at Camp Nor'wester.

By invitation, he taught during the year in the newly formed Kitanmaax School of Northwest Coast Indian Art at 'Ksan, Hazelton, B.C., where many of today's well-known Native artists would receive their original training. Among Bill's students were Freda Diesing, Walter Harris, Earl Muldoe, and Vernon Stephens.

1968–85   In the fall of 1968, Bill accepted a joint appointment at the University of Washington as curator of education at the Burke Museum, lecturer in the university's Department of Art History, and adjunct lecturer in the Department of Anthropology. This pattern of teaching continued throughout his seventeen years at the university: a sequence of three courses annually, consisting of two-dimensional Northwest Coast Native art, three-dimensional art, and the dramatic or ceremonial arts of the Northwest Coast, augmented by seminars in one or another aspect of the

Native American arts, though not always of the Northwest Coast. Class sizes grew, over the years, to as many as 250 students in his lecture courses.

At the Burke Museum, he shifted his curatorial duties, becoming curator of Northwest Coast Indian Art. At the university, in 1974, he was named full professor of art history and adjunct professor of anthropology.

1969–72    On the beach at Camp Nor'wester, he carved four monumental totem replicas for the Burke Museum, two of which now stand outside its main entrance.

1971    At the dedication of the reconstructed Chief Scow House at the Pacific Science Center in Seattle, the name *Tłalelitła* (Continually inviting) was given to Bill by Kwakwa̱ka̱'wakw Chiefs Bill Scow, Henry Bell, and Joe Seaweed.

1972    At Bill's invitation, a group of Kwakwa̱ka̱'wakw gathered on Vancouver Island to record a soundtrack for the Curtis film, now re-titled *In the Land of the War Canoes*. The restored film became commercially available the following year.

At a potlatch, daughter Carla was given the Princess Platform privilege, with its accompanying song and its name *La̱lxsa̱ndalaokwa* (Copper breaker woman) by Helen Knox.

1974    Daughter Karen was given the name *Tłexsa̱mala* by Dorothy Hawkins.

1976    He received the Washington State Governor's Art award.

A year-long fellowship from the National Endowment for the Humanities enabled him to travel to Britain, throughout Western Europe, Czechoslovakia, Scandinavia, and to Leningrad (now St. Petersburg, Russia) locating and photographing hundreds of Northwest Coast Native art objects in public and private collections. This extensive inventory laid an indispensable foundation for subsequent work by other art historians.

1977    He received the Washington State Governor's Writer's Award for *Form and Freedom: A Dialogue on Northwest Coast Indian Art* (written with Bill Reid).

1981    He received a third Washington State Governor's Writer's Award, for *Edward S. Curtis in the Land of the War Canoes: A Pioneer Cinematographer* (written with George Irving Quimby).

1983    He curated three shows: *Prancing They Come*, at the Burke Museum; *Smoky Top: The Art and Times of Willie Seaweed*, at the Pacific Science Center; and *The Box of Daylight: Northwest Coast Indian Art*, at the Seattle Art Museum.

He received the *Pacific Northwest Magazine* Award.

He received the King County Arts Commission Arts Service Award.

He received "Best of Show" award in the Technical Publications Competition, Society for Technical Communication.

1984   He received a Special Award at the Washington State Governor's Writers' Day.

1985   For the Burke Museum's centennial, he completed a carving, begun in the 1970s, of the replica of a large sculpture of a killer whale (the original is a 19<sup>th</sup>-century grave monument in Howkan, Alaska), which sits at the Burke's entrance and served, from 1985 to 1996, as the museum's logo.

He retired from his formal teaching and curatorial duties at the university in June of this year, at age sixty, to devote his time to painting, consulting, and lecturing; he was appointed curator emeritus at the Burke, and professor emeritus in the Departments of Art History and Anthropology.

1988   He received a fourth Washington State Governor's Writer's Award, for *Spirit and Ancestor: A Century of Northwest Coast Art in the Burke Museum.*

1991   He was given the Lifetime Achievement Award by fellow scholars in the Native American Art Studies Association.

1992   He received the Artistic and Cultural Achievement Award of the American Society of Interior Designers.

1993   He attended a painting workshop in Texas conducted by Howard Terpning, whom Bill regards as being foremost among western illustrators.

1994   He received the Distinguished Achievement Award of the College of Arts and Sciences at the University of Washington.

# BIBLIOGRAPHY

## BOOKS

1965   *Northwest Coast Indian Art: An Analysis of Form.* Thomas Burke Memorial Washington State Museum, Monograph No. 1. Seattle: University of Washington Press.

1972   *Crooked Beak of Heaven: Masks and Other Ceremonial Art of the Northwest Coast.*

Index of Art in the Pacific Northwest, Number 3. Seattle: University of Washington Press.

1975    *Form and Freedom: A Dialogue on Northwest Coast Indian Art* (with Bill Reid). Houston: Institute for the Arts, Rice University. Re-issued and re-titled in 1976. *Indian Art of the Northwest Coast: A Dialogue on Craftsmanship and Aesthetics*. Distributed by the University of Washington Press.

1980    *Edward S. Curtis in the Land of the War Canoes: A Pioneer Cinematographer in the Pacific Northwest* (with George Irving Quimby). Thomas Burke Memorial Washington State Museum, Monograph No. 2. Seattle: University of Washington Press.

1982    *Soft Gold: The Fur Trade and Cultural Exchange on the Northwest Coast of America* (with Thomas Vaughn). Portland: Oregon Historical Society Press.

1983a    *Smoky-Top: The Art and Times of Willie Seaweed*. Thomas Burke Memorial Washington State Museum, Monograph No. 3. Seattle: University of Washington Press.

1983b    *The Box of Daylight: Northwest Coast Indian Art*. In association with the Seattle Art Museum. Seattle: University of Washington Press.

1987    *Spirit and Ancestor: A Century of Northwest Coast Art at the Burke Museum*. Seattle: University of Washington Press.


## FILMS

1973a    *The Kwakiutl of British Columbia*. A film made in 1930 by Franz Boas. Restored and re-issued, with notes by Bill Holm. Seattle: University of Washington Press.

1973b    *In the Land of the War Canoes*. A film made in 1914 by Edward S. Curtis, originally titled *In the Land of the Head-Hunters*. Restored and re-issued, with soundtrack directed by Bill Holm. Seattle: University of Washington Press.

1980    *The Image Maker and the Indian* (with George Irving Quimby). Seattle: University of Washington Press.


## ARTICLES

1956    "Making a Blanket Capote." *American Indian Hobbyist* 3:2–4.

1958    "Plains Indian Cloth Dresses." *American Indian Hobbyist* 4:43–47.

1959a    "Crow Hair Styles and Hair Ornaments." *American Indian Hobbyist* 5:53–54.

1959b    "Crow Breechclouts." *American Indian Hobbyist* 5:59.

1961    "Carving a Kwakiutl Canoe." *The Beaver: Magazine of the North*. Summer.

1967    "The Northern Style: A Form Analysis." In *Arts of the Raven*. Vancouver: Vancouver Art Gallery.

1972    "Heraldic Carving Styles of the Northwest Coast." In *American Indian Art: Form and Tradition*. Walker Art Center, Minneapolis Institute of Arts. New York: Dutton.

1974a    "Structure and Design." In William Sturtevant, editor, *Boxes and Bowls: Decorated Containers by Nineteenth-Century Haida, Tlingit, Bella Bella, and Tsimshian Artists*. Washington, D.C.: Smithsonian Institution Press.

1974b    "The Art of Willie Seaweed: A Kwakiutl Master." In Miles Richardson, editor, *The Human Mirror: Material and Spatial Images of Man*. Baton Rouge: Louisiana University Press.

1976    "A Cannibal in the National Museum: The Early Career of Franz Boas in America" (with Curtis Hinsley). *American Anthropologist* 78:306–16.

1977    "Traditional and Contemporary Southern Kwakiutl Winter Dance." *Arctic Anthropology* 4 (1).

1978    "Die Hamatsa-Masken der Kwakiutl." *Europaische Kunstzeitschrift*. February.

1980    "American Indian Hide Painting." In *Plains Indian Design Symbology and Decoration*. Proceedings of the Third Annual Plains Indian Art Symposium.

1981a    "The Crow-Nez Perce Otter Skin Bowcase-Quiver." *American Indian Art Magazine* 6 (4).

1981b    "Will the Real Charles Edenshaw Please Stand Up?" In Donald Abbott, editor, *The World Is as Sharp as a Knife: An Anthology in Honor of Wilson Duff*. Victoria: British Columbia Provincial Museum.

1982a    "On Making Horn Bows." In T. M. Hamilton, *Native American Bows*. Columbia: Missouri Archaeological Society Press.

1982b    "A Wooling Mantle Neatly Wrought: The Early Historic Record of Northwest Coast Pattern-Twined Textiles, 1774–1850." *American Indian Art Magazine* 7 (4).

1983    "Form in Northwest Coast Indian Art." In Roy Carlson, editor, *Indian Art Traditions of the Northwest Coast*. Burnaby: Simon Fraser University.

1984    "Crow-Plateau Beadword: An Effort Toward a Uniform Terminology." *Crow Indian Art*. Chandler Institute. Pierre, South Dakota.

1985    "Old Photos Might Not Lie, but They Fib a Lot about Color." *American Indian Art Magazine* 10 (3).

1986    "The Dancing Headdress Frontlet: Aesthetic Context on the Northwest Coast." In Edwin Wade, editor, *The Arts of the North American Indian: Native Traditions in Evolution*. In association with Philbrook Art Institute. New York: Hudson Hills Press.

1987    "The Head Canoe." In Peter Corey, editor, *Faces, Voices, and Dreams: A Celebration of the Centennial of the Sheldon Jackson Museum*. Sitka: Sheldon Jackson Museum.

1988a    "Art and Culture Change at the Tlingit-Eskimo Border." In William Fitzhugh and Aron Crowell, editors, *Crossroads of Continents: Cultures of Siberia and Alaska*. Washington, D.C.: Smithsonian Institution Press.

1988b    "Cultural Exchange Across the Gulf of Alaska: Eighteenth-Century Tlingit and Pacific Eskimo Art in Spain." In José Peset, editor, *Culturas de la Costa Noroeste de America*. Madrid: Turner Libros.

1990a "Kwakiutl Winter Ceremonial." In *Handbook of North American Indians* (William C. Sturtevant, general editor), vol. 7, *Northwest Coast* (Wayne Suttles, volume editor). Washington, D.C.: Smithsonian Institution Press.

1990b "Art." In *Handbook of North American Indians* (William C. Sturtevant, general editor), vol. 7, *Northwest Coast* (Wayne Suttles, volume editor). Washington, D.C.: Smithsonian Institution Press.

1990c "The Newcombe Kwakiutl Collection of the Peabody Museum." In Barbara Isaac, editor, *The Hall of the North American Indian*. Cambridge, Mass.: Peabody Museum Press.

1991 "Historical Salish Canoes." In Robin Wright, editor, *A Time of Gathering: Native Heritage in Washington State*. Thomas Burke Memorial Washington State Museum, Monograph No. 7. Seattle: Burke Museum/Seattle: University of Washington Press.

1992 "Four Bears' Shirt: Some Problems with the Smithsonian Institution Catlin Collection." In *Artifacts/Artifakes: The Proceedings of the 1984 Plains Indian Seminar*. Cody: Buffalo Bill Historical Center.

1994 "A Gros Ventre Outfit in the C. M. Russell Museum." *Russell's West* 2 (2).

1997a "Variations on a Theme: Northern Northwest Coast Painted Boxes." *American Indian Art Magazine* 22 (2).

1997b "Northwest Coast Art at the Cheney Cowles Museum." In *Earth & Sky: Indian Art of the Americas from the Collection of the Cheney Cowles Museum*. Spokane: Cheney Cowles Museum.

1999a "Function in Northwest Coast Indian Art." In *Espíritus del Agua: Arte de Alaska y la Columbia Británica*. Barcelona, Spain: Fundació "la Caixa."

1999b "The Northwest Coast." In *Indian Summer: The First Nations of North America*. Brussels, Belgium: Royal Museums of Art and History.

# FOREWORDS TO BOOKS

1982 *The Chilkat Dancing Blanket*, by Cheryl Samuel. Seattle: Pacific Search Press.

1985 *Edward S. Curtis: The Life and Times of a Shadow Catcher*, by Barbara Davis. San Francisco: Chronicle Books.

1991 *Coast Salish Canoes*, by Leslie Lincoln. Seattle: Center for Wooden Boats.

1991 *Native American Beadwork: Traditional Beading Techniques for the Modern-Day Beadworker*, by Georg J. Barth. Stevens Point, Wis.: R. Schneider, Publishers.

1992 *Kwakiutl String Figures*, by Julia Averkieva and Mark Sherman. Seattle: University of Washington Press.

# REVIEWS OF BOOKS

1961    *Indian Primitive*, by Ralph W. Andrews. In *Oregon Historical Quarterly*. June.

1964    *Monuments in Cedar*, by Edward Keithan. In *Oregon Historical Quarterly*. June.

1970a   *Art of the Kwakiutl Indians and Other Northwest Coast Tribes*, by Audrey Hawthorn.
        In *Canadian Geographical Journal*. June.

1970b   *North American Indian Art*, by Erna Seibert and W. Forman. In *American Anthro-
        pologist*. April.

1972    *American Indian Art*, by Norman Feder. In *Pacific Search*. February.

1973    *Out of the Silence*, by Bill Reid and Adelaide de Menil. In *Pacific Search*. February.

1978a   *The Mouth of Heaven: An Introduction to Kwakiutl Religious Thought*, by Irving
        Goldman. In *Ethnohistory*.

1978b   *Objects of Bright Pride: Northwest Coast Indian Art from the American Museum
        of Natural History*, by Allen Wardwell. In *American Indian Art Magazine* 3 (2).

1983    *The Vanishing Race and Other Illusions: Photographs of Indians by Edward S.
        Curtis*, by Christopher Lyman. In *American Indian Art Magazine* 8 (1).

1989    *The Raven's Tail*, by Cheryl Samuel. In *American Indian Art Magazine* 14 (1).

1994    *The American Indian Parfleche: A Tradition of Abstract Painting*, by Gaylord
        Torrence. In *Native Arts Council Newsletter*. Seattle Art Museum. November.

# UNPUBLISHED PAPERS

1969    "The Trade Gun as a Factor in Northwest Coast Indian Art." Annual Meeting of the
        Northwest Anthropological Conference. Victoria, B.C.

1975    "Some More Conundrums in Northwest Coast Indian Art: A Kwakiutl Mask,
        Northern Carved Bowls, and More on the Copper." Symposium on Traditions and
        New Perspectives of Northwest Coast Art. University of California at Los Angeles.

1978    "Artifaking: Perception Enhancement by Doing." Annual Meeting of the American
        Anthropological Association. Los Angeles, California.

1987    "The Quill-Wrapped Horsehair Shirt." Eleventh Annual Plains Indian Seminar.
        Buffalo Bill Historical Center. Cody, Wyoming.

1990    "Recollections of Mungo Martin."

1991    "Hamsamala: The Man Eater Mask Dance of the Kwakiutl." Traditions and Inno-
        vations in Northwest Coast Indian Art. American Museum of Natural History,
        New York.

# ARTICLES ABOUT BILL HOLM

1986    Roger Downey, "The Teacher Who Taught the Experts: How a Seattle High School Teacher Unlocked the Secret of Northwest Coast Indian Art." *Historical Preservation*, September/October.

1989    Deloris Tarzan Ament, "Sharing the Form," *Seattle Times*, April 2, pp. D1 ff.

1992    Robin Wright, "Bill Holm Receives NAASA Honor Award," *Native American Art Studies Association Newsletter* 8 (2):2–5.

1996    Robin Wright, "Holm, [Oscar William] Bill." *Dictionary of Art*, vol. 14:688–89. London: Macmillan.

1999    "Bill Holm: Peintre-Ethnographie d'Aujourd'hui." *De Facto Art Magazine* (20): 10–12.

# EXHIBITIONS OF PAINTINGS AND DRAWINGS

1990    *Ate He Ye Lo — So Says the Father.* "Prix Dakota II." High Plains Heritage Center. Spearfish, South Dakota; traveled in South Dakota, 1990–91.

1992    "Indians of the Plains, Plateau, and Northwest Coast: Paintings by Bill Holm." Burke Museum, University of Washington.

1992    "Recent Paintings by Bill Holm." Stonington Gallery. Seattle, Washington.

1993    *A Chief by Means of Deeds.* "American Miniatures." Settlers West Gallery. Tucson, Arizona.

1995    *Oh Yes! I Love You, Honey Dear.* "American Miniatures." Settlers West Gallery. Tucson, Arizona.

1996    *The Buffalo Runner* and *The Coup Counter.* "American Miniatures." Settlers West Gallery. Tucson, Arizona.

1999    *Hoylik̲ala̱* "Indian Summer." Royal Museums of Art and History. Brussels, Belgium.

# PUBLISHED PAINTINGS AND DRAWINGS

1956    *Nez Perce Scout.* In *The Beaver: Magazine of the North*, August, cover; also in *Appaloosa News*, November 1961, cover; also in *The Western Horseman Calendar*, 1966.

1958    *Crow Trailing Horses*. In *The Western Horseman*, June, cover.

1961    *Kwakiutl Canoes*. In *The Beaver: Magazine of the North*, Summer, cover; also in Kenneth G. Roberts and Philip Shackleton, *The Canoe: A History of the Craft from Panama to the Arctic*, Toronto: Macmillan of Canada, 1983; also in *Alaskafest*, Alaska Airlines Magazine, May 1984.

1971    [Untitled painting]. In David Richardson, *Pig War Islands*. Eastsound, Wash.: Orcas Publishing, cover.

1987    *Potlatch Guests Arriving at Sitka*. Friends of Sheldon Jackson Museum poster; also in Peter Corey, editor, *Faces, Voices, and Dreams*, 1987, color, double page; also in Edmund Carpenter, editor, *Materials for the Study of Social Symbolism in Ancient & Tribal Art: A Record of Tradition & Continuity, Based on the Researches & Writings of Carl Schuster* 2 (3):668. New York: Rock Foundation, 1988, black-and-white; also in James Cassidy, editor, *Through Indian Eyes*, 1995, color, double page.

1988    "Cultural Exchange Across the Gulf of Alaska: Eighteenth-Century Tlingit and Pacific Eskimo Art in Spain." In José Peset, editor, *Culturas de la Noroeste de America*. Line drawings, figures 14–24, detailing designs on Northwest Coast objects pictured in the accompanying article.

1991a   *Raven Warrior*. Limited edition print; also in *American Indian Art Magazine* 18 (4).

1991b   *Approach to Tsakhees*. Note card; also in *De Facto Art Magazine*, 1999 (20): 12, color.

1991c   *Parade*. Limited edition print.

1992a   *Going Visiting*. Burke Museum poster.

1995    *Ha̱msa̱mala*. Limited edition print; note card; also in *De Facto Art Magazine*, 1999 (20): 12, color.

1995    *Sea Otter Dart*. In James Cassidy, editor, *Through Indian Eyes*, color.

1996    *The Decision*. In Paul L. Hedren, *Traveler's Guide to the Great Sioux War: Battlefields, Forts, and Related Sites of America's Greatest Indian War*. Helena: Montana Historical Society Press, cover.

1997    In Steven C. Brown, *Native Visions: Evolution in Northwest Coast Art from the Eighteenth through the Twentieth Century*. Line drawings detailing designs on Northwest Coast objects pictured on pages 12, 17, and 18.

1999a   *Hoylika̱la̱ɫ*. In *Indian Summer: Les Premiers Nations de l'Amerique du Nord*. Brussels, Belgium: Royal Museums of Art and History. Full-page color on page 80; also in *Voyager Magazine*, No. 96.

1999b   *The Spanish Broadsword, Purifying the Shield, Approach to Tsakhees*, and *Ha̱msa̱mala*. In *De Facto Art Magazine* (20).

1999c   *Raven Warriors*. In *Spring/Summer Catalog*, University of Washington Press, cover.